THE PSYCHIC WITHIN

THE
PSYCHIC
WITHIN

TRUE PSYCHIC STORIES

DAYLE SCHEAR
PSYCHIC

Blue Dolphin Publishing
1994

Also by Dayle Schear:

Dare to Be Different!
Tarot for the Beginner
What If? (forthcoming)

Copyright © 1994 ESP & Me Inc.
All rights reserved.

Published by Blue Dolphin Publishing, Inc.
P.O. Box 1920, Nevada City, CA 95959

Orders: 1 (800) 643-0765

ISBN# 0-931892-90-2

Library of Congress Cataloging-in-Publication Data

Schear, Dayle.
    The psychic within : true psychic stories / Dayle Schear.
      p.   cm.
    ISBN 0-931892-90-2 : $14.95
    1. Schear, Dayle.   2. Psychics—United States—Biography.
I. Title.
BF1027.S34A3 1994
133.8'092—dc20   94-3987
[B]   CIP

Cover art: Sharon Hartman

Printed in the United States of America by
Blue Dolphin Press, Inc., Grass Valley, California

10   9   8   7   6   5   4   3   2   1

Welcome to My World of E.S.P.
Let me take you for a ride
into the mind, body and spirit!
of a Psychic.
Turn the pages slowly,
for there's so much to learn.

PSYCHIC DAYLE SCHEAR

TELEVISION APPEARANCES

Sightings FOX (National Telecast)
Hard Copy Magazine (National Telecast)
New Year TV Special (FUJI-TV Tokyo, Japan-National)
Hour Magazine CBS (National Telecast)
The Late Show FOX (National Telecast)
AM San Francisco KGO-ABC (Regular 1 Year)
2 At Noon KTVU (Oakland)
ESP & You One Hour Specials (KGMB-CBS, Hawaii, 10 Yrs.)
Your Future One Hour Special (KGMB-CBS Hawaii)
Hawaiian Moving Company (KGMB-CBS Hawaii)
Anchorage Live (KIMO-ABC Alaska)
Good Morning Alaska (KIMO-ABC Alaska)
ESP & You One Hour Special (KIMO-ABC Alaska)
KHON News (NBC Hawaii)
KITV News (ABC Hawaii)
Mystical Healing (Cable 22, Hawaii)
Daytime Show (KOLO-ABC Reno)
KOLO News (ABC Reno)
KHBC (Hilo, Hawaii)
Numerous Telethons (Charities)

NIGHT CLUBS

Harrah's (Lake Tahoe & Reno, Nevada)
American Hawaii Cruise (Cruise Ship)
Holiday Inn (Waikiki, Hawaii)
23rd Step (Hawaii)

RADIO SHOWS

21st Century Radio (Syndicated Nationally);
KGO, K101, KEST, KALX (San Francisco);
**KSSK (K59), KGU, KULA, KKUA, KIKI, KCCN,
I-94, KISA, KMVI, KKON, KPUA, KAUI** (Hawaii);
KOWL, KTHO, KPTL, KLKT, (Lake Tahoe & Reno);
KENI (Alaska); **WWDB** (Philadelphia); **WCBM** (Baltimore)

ARTICLES/OTHERS

The Washington Times • Honolulu Advertiser
Honolulu Star Bulletin • Honolulu Magazine
Tahoe Tribune • Reno Gazette
The Spectator (Mass.)

ACKNOWLEDGMENTS

I wish to thank the following people for their encouragement, help, and support: my husband, Blythe; my teacher and mentor, Psychic Peter Hurkos, his wife Stephany and daughter Gloria; Doug Bushousen, who hired me for my first nightclub show at Harrah's; Barbara from Side Street Boutique, who supplied all my show clothes for Harrah's; John Parker, for my first radio show; Duane Triplett, for my first television special; the whole staff at KGMB (CBS)—Richard Grimm, Bob Turner, Laura Chee, Anita Brady, etc.; my director; Mark Williams; my assistant producers, Michelle Honda and Jamie Oshiro; "Hawaiian Moving Company," Randy Brandt, for my first television segment in Hawaii; Radio KSSK, Perry and Price; all the television and radio deejays and hosts I worked with—Mark Lennartz, Ken Hunter, Dave Lancaster, John Kealoha, Dona Baxter, Bill Thompson, etc.; Doug Bruckner; "Hard Copy Magazine"; and all the people who helped with my live shows and appearances. Special thanks to Dr. Cannon, chiropractor, who kept my back in shape while I wrote this book.

More special thanks to Phil and Esther, Alonzo, Jerry, and Bernie. I also wish to thank Mom and Dad, Mother and Father Arakawa, BJ & Fred, Laraine Yamamoto, Dr. Andrija Puharich, Mel Doerr, Beverly Lyons, David and Rachel Glyn, Karin Beals, Crissy Kengla, Dale Ogata, Aunt Molly, Gerri Williams, and Detective Steve Kibbe.

Special thanks once again to Marion and Stanley for always being there when I needed you the most.

Special thanks also to my editor, Maybelle Boyd. Looks like we did it again! I wish there were words to thank you over and over again. *The Psychic Within* was very hard and frustrating to write at times. Maybelle always encouraged me to keep writing. I'm lost for words; this special woman, Maybelle Boyd, was truly sent to me from heaven.

As a writer writes and creates special thoughts, feelings pour out from within the heart. Caught up in these special moments, at times I found my thoughts were locked up within my mind until they found their way out onto the paper without rhyme nor reason. On many given occasions I had virtually no one to turn to, to unlock my special feelings, until I found Maybelle Boyd. Through her patience and understanding, she taught me what it was like to be a writer. My thoughts flowed through her hands as she edited with kindness and understanding every word that I wrote. There are no words to thank someone who has given you so much, for without this very special editor, this book would have never been written. The special gift that Maybelle has is the ability to always know what I was thinking and also to make my words sound beautiful and touching. Although at times my grammar was not quite appropriate, I thank Maybelle for letting me be me. Thank you, Maybelle, for your countless hours, most of which came from your heart. Thanks also to Corinn Codye, for putting the finishing touches on the manuscript.

Special thanks, too, to Marvin Kooken of South Lake Tahoe Computer Base. Thanks, Marvin, for your countless hours of computer time and especially for teaching me how a computer works. If it wasn't for your kindness and relentless hours of patience, this book would have never been handed to my editor, Maybelle Boyd.

THANK YOU

TABLE OF CONTENTS

Introduction	xv
Special Thanks to My Readers	xvi
Chapter 1 • **A Meeting with Destiny**	1
Chapter 2 • **Give a Psychic a Chance**	9
Chapter 3 • **Aloha Airlines, The Quest of Flight 243**	16
Chapter 4 • **Galaxy Airlines Flight 203**	26
Chapter 5 • **Come Fly with Me**	34
Chapter 6 • **Achille Lauro**	43
Chapter 7 • **The Art of Saving Lives**	50
Chapter 8 • **It Should Only Happen to You**	67
Chapter 9 • **Experiencing the Unusual**	76
Chapter 10 • **A Child Is Missing**	95
Chapter 11 • **Lizzie Borden**	103

Chapter 12 • **The Case of Diane Suzuki**	119
Chapter 13 • ***Hard Copy* Australia**	155
Chapter 14 • **Jury Convicts Tandal**	166
Chapter 15 • **Peter Hurkos**	172
Chapter 16 • **Listen! to the Universe**	183
Chapter 17 • **Every Psychic Needs a Psychic**	193
Chapter 18 • **Psychic Surgery**	219
Chapter 19 • **Imelda Marcos**	204
Chapter 20 • **A Bizarre Request**	212
Chapter 21 • **Living with a Psychic**	234
Chapter 22 • **The Psychic Within Me**	240

This book is dedicated to my husband, **Blythe Arakawa.**

INTRODUCTION

Go ahead. Open the book. Read on. You didn't pick up this book merely by chance. You see, when the student is ready, the teacher will appear.

Come join me. Step into the mind of a Psychic for just a brief moment in time. Come see what I see, feel what I feel. Try to walk away when someone cries and says, "You're the only one who can help me." Experience my laughter and my tears.

My name is Dayle. I have stories to tell you; come along for the ride. Some people call me a Psychic. Others say I see the future. Some say I'm just plain different.

Just imagine for one moment that you are me; you are able to see right through almost anyone you come in contact with. You know each person as well as you know yourself. There are times you want to run and hide, and times you want to help. There are times you just want to give it all up. *The Psychic Within* is more than a book. It tells you how a Psychic thinks and feels.

We Psychics really aren't that different from other people, you know. We love, we hurt, we cry. To know me is to know yourself. I was sent here to guide you!

Special Thanks to My Readers

While writing my first book, *Dare to Be Different!*, I never would have imagined the pain of being a writer. I gave up so much, just for the sake of writing. **Was it all worth it?**

The first-time writer never knows if his or her work is good enough. Some writers will never find out. I was one of the lucky ones.

When my books were delivered to my home, I was in ecstasy. Shortly thereafter, panic set in. What do I do next? Are people going to like my book? Should I have changed everyone's name?

It was too late. I had given birth to my baby, and now I had to let her go. Before too long the letters and phone calls came pouring in, and they continue to come in every day. Many countless people have stopped me on the street to thank me or to tell me that they couldn't put down my book, *Dare to Be Different!*

I've included a few samplings phone calls and letters here:

"I bought your book at one o'clock in the afternoon. I started reading, and read until I fell asleep at midnight. I woke up at 2:00 a.m. with the book open on my chest, and I stayed up the rest of the night until I finished it. I couldn't put it down!"

"Thank you for sharing your life and for being so honest."

"**You** wrote this book, but you wrote about **my** life!"

"This was the **first** book I've read from **cover** to **cover** in over **twenty** years."

"Your book shows you as a real woman with the same problems as everyone else—reading your story helped me so much!"

"**. . . a real page-turner!**"

"**Dear Dayle,** Hi! I'm sure you won't remember me. I had a reading with you earlier this year, and I purchased your book *Dare to Be Different!* I enjoyed reading it. I'm not much of a reader because books put me to sleep.

"Your book was so interesting that from the time I received it I couldn't put it down. I was finished within the first week. Wow! I must say you led a very exciting life."

Aloha, Vivian

"**Dear Dayle**, Thank You! I'm no bookworm but after reading a few chapters of *Dare to Be Different!* I just couldn't put the book down. I laughed when it tickled my funny bone and shed a tear when the sad parts came around. Dayle, maybe a movie will materialize from this book!! We shall always cherish your autographed book."

Much Mahalo!! Betty

"**Dear Dayle**, I received your book *Dare to Be Different!* a few weeks back, and I'm writing to tell you I enjoyed it so much. I read it in the afternoon after I got up and read till well past midnight. I couldn't keep my eyes open anymore.

"I couldn't put the book down. A couple of weeks later I read it again. Girl, you led a crazy life! It was fantastic and funny but most of all very engrossing. You did one hell of a job writing it. Thanks for being so honest about your life."

Aloha, Eloise

Writer's Comment

I appreciate every letter, call, and comment that I get. I can't forget all the wonderful people who called me just to thank me for writing this book. Thank you all very much from the bottom of my heart.

Keep those phone calls and letters pouring in. Every letter, every phone call, is appreciated.

And to those who have judged me, thanks for reading my book anyway, for without you, *The Psychic Within* would have never materialized. You kept my fire going.

The Psychic Within

The stories you are about to read are true. Each and every story has a meaning. Turn the pages slowly, for I have a quest. I was put here on this earth to help one person in Mankind, for if I can help but one person, I will have helped a world full of souls. That one person just might be you.

The Psychic Within is about my working life. The two books together, *Dare to Be Different!* and *The Psychic Within,* tell many of the great adventures I have experienced.

Now it's time to go for a ride. Get ready for some spine-chilling stories. Remember, each and every one of these stories is true.

Some people who appear in my book are presented as composite characters. In order to protect their privacy, the sequence of some events is modified accordingly. However, all the events are true.

TRUE PSYCHIC STORIES

CHAPTER 1

A MEETING WITH DESTINY

While I was growing up back east in Newark, New Jersey, a young lady named Marlies von Laufer was growing up in another part of the world called Straubing, Bavaria, which is about sixty miles from Munich, Germany. Little did we know that in the year 1991 our paths would cross and our lives would change forever.

This is her story and, eventually, mine. When Marlies was two, her father told her that her mother had died of a rare lung disease. Many years passed before Marlies accepted the passing of her mother.

Then one day her father blurted out in anger, "Marlies, you act just like your mother. Everything you do, everything you say, annoys me and reminds me of her."

Marlies was confused. "Dad, what is it . . . why do you think I act like my mother?" she screamed.

"Because you are as stubborn as your mother!" he yelled.

That's when Marlies began to question her father. "Dad, tell me about my mother. What was she like? Why am I so much like her?"

Annoyed by the relentless questioning, her father shook Marlies and shouted, "Your mother is dead! Never mention her name in this house again!"

Marlies was extremely perceptive; she read between the lines. Her father's tone of voice made her aware that there was something more.

Then the visionary dreams began. And in those visions, her mother would motion to her and say, *"Marlies, come back to me. My child, please come back to me."* There was no end to these repetitive dreams, which haunted her for years to come.

About twenty-five years later Marlies recalled a major incident at her grandmother's funeral that reconfirmed her thinking about her mother's death.

She recalled Ingrid, her sister, standing by her side during the funeral. Suddenly, for no apparent reason, Ingrid blurted out angrily, *"You think you know everything. Well, I have news for you. Our mother is alive and she has remarried! What do you think of that?"*

Marlies was outraged. She lunged at her sister and shook her violently. "Tell me the truth," she shouted. "What do you mean, our mother is alive?"

Ingrid remained silent, then broke away from Marlies' vice-like grip and raced toward the car.

Marlies ran toward her father, screaming, "Dad, Dad, Ingrid said that Mother is still alive! Why did she say that?"

Her father shook his finger at Marlies. "I don't know why, but I'll find out. I told you, your mother is dead. How can you bring this up at your grandmother's funeral? You should be ashamed of yourself! Now be still; I don't want to hear another word from you." He spoke with a heavy, harsh German accent.

The funeral ended. Marlies' father huddled closely to her sister, whispering softly while he questioned her. Then Ingrid denied every word and snickered at Marlies. That was the last time Marlies would speak to her sister.

With the passing of years, Marlies' visions and dreams grew ever stronger. The vision of her mother reaching out her hand and saying, *"My child, come back to me,"* grew so much clearer.

Marlies knew there was something more to what her sister had said. The reaction of her father was a dead giveaway. So, she launched a search for her mother through every relative known to her. The search spanned well over thirty-five years. Yet, the answers always remained the same: "Your mother is dead!"

But Marlies never gave up hope. She knew that someday she would find her mother. Little did she know that day was just about to happen.

A meeting with destiny was at hand. It was June, 1991. Marlies and I both now resided in the Hawaiian Islands. Fate was just about to throw the two of us together.

I recall it was a hot summer day in Honolulu when Marlies arrived at my door. A set of unusual circumstances was about to occur.

First, Marlies' friend had booked an appointment with me and was *unable* to keep her appointment.

Second, by chance, Marlies decided to take her friend's appointment.

Third, destiny had thrown the two of us together.

I politely introduced myself to Marlies and asked her to sit down and relax. I asked if I could hold a piece of jewelry that she was wearing. She handed me her ring, then her watch. I held them tightly in my hands, waiting for the visions to come. Within moments, my words were flowing out to Marlies.

I started off by describing where Marlies lived as a child in Germany. I described in detail all about her childhood. Marlies interrupted me with a question.

"Dayle, I want to know how my mother died."

I paused for a moment to gather my thoughts. I stared into space while holding her jewelry. The visions I saw in my mind's eye startled me.

I spoke rapidly. It seemed as though I were channeling information directly to her.

"Marlies, your mother is alive! She's in Germany. She's been waiting all these years for you to find her. I see her by water. She looks out of a window and gazes over the water and thinks of you. She waits patiently for you to call.

"You have two half-sisters. Your mother walks with a limp. She knows someday you'll find her.

"She waits for you to call her Mama. If you search for her in Germany as you would search for gold, you surely will find your mother." Breathless, I stopped. A feeling of exhaustion came over me.

Marlies screamed. "I was told my mother was dead! What you're telling me—how can this be?"

"I don't know, Marlies. All I know is your mother is alive. Find a way to locate her and, when you do, let me know," I said.

Marlies left my house, dazed. There was something in my voice, something in that reading, that made sense to her. Marlies believed every word.

More than a month passed.

My phone rang. "Dayle, this is Marlies. Remember me? I'm the one who was searching for my mother."

Her voice quivered with excitement. "Dayle, I found her! I FOUND MY MOTHER! How can I thank you, Dayle?"

Now it was my turn. Tears came to my eyes. I paused to regain my composure before responding.

"Marlies, you don't have to thank me," I said. "How did you find your mother?"

"Thanks to you, when I left your house I was convinced that my mother was alive. I called my stepmother in Germany and explained to her that I had been to a Psychic. She believes in Psychics and was extremely interested in what I had to say. I explained to her what you told me, that my mother was alive. I caught her off guard. When my stepmother regained her composure, she spoke very cautiously.

" 'Marlies,' she said, 'to tell you the truth, I know your mother didn't die when you were two years old. This is very hard for me to say. . . . I know she remarried, but I don't know if she is still alive today. If anyone would know where she is, it would be your cousin. You contact your cousin; he seems to keep track of all our relatives.'

" 'My cousin! I have a cousin?' I asked in amazement.

" 'Yes, here is the number; call him!' she said.

"After several attempts for over a month, I finally reached my cousin. When I made contact, I explained about the Psychic reading. My cousin abruptly said he would check things out and call me back in a few hours.

"Approximately four hours later I was sitting by the phone, waiting patiently for my cousin to call. When he finally called, he blurted out, *'Marlies, here's your mother's telephone number.'* Then he slammed the phone in my ear.

"I was shocked; my nerves were rattled. I dialed the number slowly, with excitement and fear. The telephone rang and rang. My mother finally picked up the phone. 'Hello,' she said in a sweet, caring voice.

" 'Mama, Mama, this is . . .'

" 'I know!' she interrupted. 'Marlies, my little Marlies. It's you, my child; it's really you!'

"When she heard my voice, she knew I was her daughter. Mama said, 'I've waited a lifetime to hear your voice! I've waited for years to hear you call me Mama! I knew you'd find me before I die.'

"Tears ran down my cheeks as I cried out, *'Mama, it's you, it's really you! It took forty years to find you.'* "

Destiny had played its hand; the meeting was almost complete.

As for Marlies, hard financial times were upon her. She couldn't afford the price of a plane ticket to Germany. However, after several phone calls to her mother, she somehow found a way.

Her first meeting with her mother was on October 6, 1991, in Germany. When Marlies finally met with her, it seemed as if time stood still. The reunion began. Marlies found out she had two stepsisters, just as I had stated. Her mother had a trailer that Marlies' stepfather and she went camping in on many occasions. This trailer was on a parcel of land that overlooked the water.

Marlies learned that her mother used to gaze out of the kitchen window, looking out over the water, hoping her daughter would come back to her. I had mentioned that her mother walked with a limp, and she did; she had bruised her foot just recently.

Marlies asked her mother why she had left her. Her mother responded, "I never left you willingly. When I came back from the war, your father accused me of fooling around. He cast me out, never to see my children again. I was banned from my own home and family. I was dead in your father's eyes, and the family was forbidden to speak of me."

Marlies bent her head in shame. "Oh, Mama, I'm so sorry for what he did," she said. But nothing else mattered any more. Marlies had found her mother; the reunion was complete. The missing part of her life was now a complete chapter.

The concluding words Marlies spoke to me were, "Thank you, Dayle, for giving me back my life."

A Brief Explanation

I can only ponder how this event occurred!

Marlies von Laufer came to me looking for answers. With one touch of her jewelry (a psychic method called *psychometry:* to touch personal objects to see into the past, present, or future), I found myself taken back forty years. The visions grew stronger and stronger. Simultaneously, I became intensely aware of her mother, the very person I was trying to locate somewhere in Germany. Once my mind fixed upon her mother's mind, we were able to create a bond of *telepathy,* or mind-to-mind contact. When I saw in my mind her mother gazing out of the window, I knew she was still alive.

My thoughts raced toward her mother with such a rapid intensity that, at that moment, the mother sensed Marlies trying to find her through me. I now had to figure out the best route for Marlies to find her mother. With her mind wide open, Marlies' mother unintentionally sent telepathic signals to the family for help in finding her daughter. All our minds had to be receptive for such a linkage to occur, and for just one split moment, all our minds became one. But it was only through Marlies' endless pursuit that she was finally able to find her mother.

You see, the Psychic can see the future and the events that may occur. However, if Marlies had waited and ignored the situation, the thought pattern would have dissipated. She would never have located her mother. *A Psychic can see, but it is always up to the individual to pursue the matter.*

Marlies first spoke with her mother by phone on August 12, 1991. She flew to Germany to meet with her mother for the very first time on October 6, 1991.

Exactly one year later, *October 6, 1992,* her mother died of cancer in Marlies' arms in Germany.

They had one priceless year to learn all about each other. Marlies found not only her mother, but many other loving relatives as well.

I asked Marlies, "Was it worth it?"

"Yes, Dayle, it was," she replied. "I found the missing part of me through my mother. Although our time together was short, every moment we spent together was worth it. Dayle, you gave me back my life."

Marlies and I have remained friends ever since.

CHAPTER 2

GIVE A PSYCHIC A CHANCE

"We're live on the radio with self-proclaimed Psychic Dayle Schear," the reporter announced. "When did you discover that you were Psychic?" he asked me. "Have you been Psychic all your life?"

Before I could answer, the reporter interjected, "Who's going to be the next President? If you're so Psychic, tell me something about me."

I stared at the reporter. "You want me to tell you something about you?" I asked.

"Yes," he replied smugly.

I held his hand tightly. The anger inside me began to stir. My thoughts raced back in time and the visions began. We made eye contact. The words started pouring out of me. "Do you really want to know?" I squeezed his hand tighter and tighter.

"Yes, go on. Say something. Don't hold back. I have nothing to hide."

"You have nothing to hide," I thought out loud. "Sir, might I remind you that we all have skeletons in our closet."

"I'm not afraid," he replied. "You Psychics speak in generalities anyway."

That was the straw that broke this Psychic's back. I didn't want

9

to humiliate him. My ability was my only weapon to fight off such an attack. "You, sir, are very arrogant and insecure," I began.

"That's exactly what I mean—generalities. Can't you Psychics say something specific? Tell me the license plate number of my car. What's my address?" He spoke tauntingly.

Why did it always have to come to this? I thought. *Why don't they understand?* I didn't want to degrade him, but he left me no choice.

"I see. You want something specific?" I responded calmly. "Do you want me to tell the listening audience about your dishonorable discharge from the Navy? Or would you rather I tell the listeners how you slap your wife around? Or how you hospitalized your daughter last year? Or do you . . ."

"Stop!" he shouted. "Who told you? You must have spoken to one of my friends."

I continued. "You had a sister who committed suicide, and you're scared the same thing will happen to you. Do you want to know when you're going to die?"

"Stop!" he yelled. "That's enough! I'll get to the bottom of this. I'll find out who told you, and I'll expose you."

I smiled and said, "But they're only generalities. Why are you getting so upset?" I released my knuckle grip from his hand.

I was angry. My thoughts were ablaze. *Why does it have to come to this? Why can't people just accept what I do? Why do they always think there is a trick involved? I give up!*

I stood up abruptly and headed for the door. I glanced back. The phone lines were all lit up. I shook my head in outrage.

The life of a Psychic isn't easy. You spend half of your life convincing people that you are real. It isn't as though I don't have a skill or trade. I guess in the end, the good outweighs the bad. I sometimes have to remind myself that for every person who doesn't believe in ESP, there are many people out there who do, that every soul I help in return helps many other souls.

This was a turning point in my life. I could believe what that deranged reporter was saying to me and give it all up. Or, I could choose to rise above the situation and ignore him and everyone like him. I chose the latter.

The negative, ignorant attitude of this particular reporter seems to be the general opinion of some people concerning Psychics. Granted, there are many Psychics who are "out to lunch." This situation, of course, does not reflect the whole. There are also many Psychics who are good. Unfortunately, we don't have a reliable device to measure ESP. If there were such a device, one could eliminate the inadequate Psychics from the good ones. The main reason Psychic ability can't be measured is that the whole basis of how it works deals with feelings and emotions. For example, one can't measure love. There are no devices to measure feelings or emotions, and psychic ability is based on feelings and emotions.

Learning About Psychics

Psychics come in all shapes, colors and ethnic backgrounds.

A Psychic child knows that he or she is different from other children and tends to live in a fantasy world where all beliefs are possible. Dreams or visions will occur repeatedly. These dreams or visions tend to materialize in the future. The passing of years seems to mature the Psychic:

- Telepathy begins to develop.

- Transference of thought or reading of the mind becomes a natural part of adulthood.
- The Psychic matures. To learn how to focus, he or she picks a tool such as cards, crystals, numerology, astrology and/or psychometry. All these tools enable the Psychic to focus on the client in a reading.
- If there is a natural ability, the Psychic will tend to be obsessive about ESP, picking up every book available and reading everything about the field. With practice, the ability increases. Only the most gifted Psychics will go above and beyond this point.

I believe there is some portion of the brain that is not yet understood by science. This portion of the brain is like a muscle; the more you exercise it, the more it will develop. I believe it is present in every human being and throughout the animal kingdom.

A Psychic is similar to a radio receiver. All he or she has to do is sit back and tune in to receive impressions. When we Psychics turn on the radio and the signal is not coming in adequately, we fine tune the radio until we receive the station clearly. Until a Psychic learns to *focus* or fine tune his or her impressions, s/he gets a great deal of useless information. The moment direct contact is made, information will pass to the Psychic correctly. We call this a *link*. A Psychic needs *focus* to give a client an accurate reading.

Psychic ability takes many years to fine tune. Practice is the key. The more we practice, the more our ability increases. Psychics tend to make the most mistakes when they rely only on telepathy. This is a common mistake for well over eighty percent of all Psychics.

One thing, however, separates the men from the boys. A trained Psychic learns how to differentiate between telepathy and reality.

This is not something that comes naturally; it's only through experience and proper training that a Psychic will learn the difference. The Psychic field is unique in that the older you are and the more experiences you have had, the more your ability soars. Many times my clients have asked, "Dayle, how do you know you're not just reading my mind?" Very good question. I respond, "Through proper training and experience."

Example: In a reading the client desperately wants her lover to leave his wife and believes he will. The Psychic who only uses telepathy agrees with the client and tells her that her boyfriend will leave his wife. The client leaves the Psychic, believing that her lover will be hers shortly. Years later the client will come back to the Psychic and ask, "Why hasn't my lover left his wife?" The inexperienced Psychic won't realize what went wrong.

The same woman chooses a more experienced Psychic and asks the same question. "Will my lover leave his wife?" The experienced Psychic, using more advanced methods, tells the woman, "I'm sorry, but your lover will not leave his wife for you. It's possible that five years down the road he may leave; however, I don't see you ending up with this man." The client is devastated. She may choose to end the relationship. Hopefully, she will decide not to waste precious years of her life waiting for her lover to leave his wife.

The example I have given you is true. However, we all have free will. It's up to the client to make the final decision. I feel one should always be honest with people. As a Psychic I hold the highest code of ethics. I have a duty to my clients always to guide them on the right path. The client, however, always has the final choice.

As you can see, telepathy, or mind reading, is the foremost misunderstood word connected with ESP. Until the Psychic learns the difference between telepathy and the word *realization,* meaning what will really happen, he or she cannot hope to attain a major degree of accuracy. As such, we Psychics tend to be viewed with nonexistent credibility.

Police departments realize that Psychics tend to read minds. They believe that Psychics cannot provide additional information. Most police departments just slough off anything a Psychic says. They're tired of the mind readers of the world. When a crime is in progress, they are given virtually hundreds of leads from so-called Psychics. Most of these "leads" would lead to dead ends.

However, even though police departments have this bad taste in their mouths, every so often a Psychic comes along who is genuine and real, one who has a lot to offer. Unfortunately, because of the bad rap, the police discount most Psychic information as useless.

Example: In many instances Psychics have misled police. Or they have mainly read the detective's mind to come to the same conclusion. If the detective is wrong, so will the Psychic be wrong. The Psychic and detective get nowhere fast. The Psychic loses credibility, and the detective loses faith in the Psychic.

On the other hand, there have been cases where a Psychic has given information to the police department as to where to find a body, only to be arrested and accused of the crime.

I would hope to see in the future a day when police chiefs all over the world are receptive to working with Psychics. Detective and Psychic should train together. I hope there will come a time in the future when the headlines of the newspaper will read, *Detective and Psychic help solve murder.*

The best way to rule out inexperienced and phony Psychics is through education. In choosing a Psychic, make sure that the person comes highly recommended.

Prices for a Psychic will vary from $20 up to $500 per reading. However, remember, you don't always get what you pay for. Price is created solely by the Psychics themselves. The more in demand a Psychic is, the higher the price. The reason for this is not greed. Psychics have a burnout point; they can see only so many people per day. When Psychics are in demand, virtually hundreds of people want to see them. When Psychics do an abundance of readings, it is a known fact that their health tends to deteriorate at a very rapid pace. Their high price is usually set so that they are not flooded with readings to the point of burnout.

Beware of Psychics who say they will remove a curse from you.

Beware of Psychics who tell you to give them more money while in a reading. This is very unprofessional. The fee should be set in the beginning.

Beware of Psychics who tell you evil spirits are lurking around you or that you are an unlucky person. This ploy is used to get more money from the client.

Beware of Psychics who give you lucky numbers for the lottery and tell you that you will win. If this were true, the Psychics would use the lucky numbers for themselves and become rich.

Beware of Psychics who tell you of your death. This is a scare tactic for more money.

I believe everyone has ESP, whether they realize it or not. Sometimes people call it intuition. Others claim it's lady luck. ESP is all of that and more. There are gifted singers and artists who excel in life. There are gifted Psychics as well. A good Psychic will help guide you and tell you your options in the future.

A professional Psychic will help you to help yourself. A professional Psychic will always tell you the truth, not just what you want to hear. The greatest injustice in life is to lead people on. Truth is always the answer.

In my opinion—if only the radio reporter could have understood—sometimes it's worth your time to give a Psychic a chance.

CHAPTER 3

ALOHA AIRLINES
THE QUEST OF FLIGHT 243

January, 1988. Exactly three months before the Aloha Airlines Flight 243 disaster would occur, the fortune teller looked upon my face with horror.

She held the palm of my hand tightly; her visions grew intense. I started to pull my hand away. "No!" she said. "Wait! I see a vision of a plane going down. The plane is falling . . . it's losing altitude . . . it's heading toward the ocean. It looks like an Outer Island, or maybe Japan." I started squirming. She continued, "There's a problem with the plane!" I pulled my hand away abruptly. "You will survive. You will live. Don't worry; it will be okay."

Well, I thought, here we go again! My weakness—a cup of tea, a regular visit to a metaphysical book shop, and off to see your local fortune teller.

I was in Hilo when the fortune teller told me of this vision. I sank deeper and deeper into my chair. My eyes were wide open. I gasped for air. I was in the midst of my Outer Island tour, and Hilo was my last stop. A mutual friend had introduced me to this fortune teller. I had heard she was quite good, but just an amateur.

My husband Blythe sat by my side as the fortune teller rambled on. He angrily interrupted the reading. "You must be picking up on

Dayle's fear of flying. This can't be true!" he shouted. "I understand how ESP works. You must be misinterpreting what you see; besides, it's cruel to say these things," he cautioned the fortune teller. "Where is your code of ethics? Don't you know these things scare people? You can damage their thinking mentally." Infuriated, Blythe began to stare down the fortune teller; his eyes pierced directly into hers. If looks could kill. . . !

I sat in the corner of the room, listening intently, waiting for the fortune teller to speak. Blythe didn't want me to listen anymore. "That's the difference between a Psychic and a fortune teller, Dayle: one is a professional, the other is an amateur," Blythe said as he grabbed my arm. "Come on, Dayle, we're leaving. Enough of this; she's just an amateur."

The fortune teller stared in his direction. "You, young man, listen! There will be a death in your family," she mumbled proudly.

Blythe and I continued walking rapidly. He slammed the door behind him. We walked in silence. My mind was churning. I somehow don't take these things lightly. I was trying to figure out what the fortune teller was really saying.

Because of all my years of experience, I know that a Psychic can misinterpret certain things. I was beginning to wonder. Maybe, just maybe, she wasn't picking up on the past. Maybe this could happen, but I figured there wasn't anything I could do about it. You can't change your own destiny, I thought. Or can you?

My thought pattern drifted further. If I was aware of a plane disaster, I could try to avoid it. The disaster might still occur, but I didn't have to be on that plane. This much I knew!

I also knew how Blythe felt about this situation; I didn't want to question him. We continued on with our Outer Island tour. All went well and we reached Honolulu safely.

Three months later I ran into one of my friends, Michelle Honda. Michelle is a flight attendant for Aloha Airlines. We usually saw each other in passing, since her schedule was quite erratic. Michelle was dating a fellow by the name of Phil, who was the producer of my television show, *ESP & You*. I was surprised to see her. I asked Michelle about her schedule for the following weekend. As far as she knew, they were free, so I invited them to my house for dinner.

"Great!" Michelle replied. "We'll have a wonderful time; we can catch up on things. See you next week Sunday."

April 24, 1988. We were sitting around talking and having fun. That evening was special. I asked Michelle if she wanted a Psychic reading. Politely, she said, "No, Dayle, but I would love for you to give Phil a reading. Why don't the two of you go outside. I'll make the salad, and you can toss Phil around psychically." She giggled.

We had a wonderful dinner and played some inventive board games. I noticed that the evening was just a little bit different because, in the past, whenever Michelle and Phil came to my house, Michelle was always the first one to ask for a reading. This time she seemed to be more concerned with Phil; Phil was searching for new and brighter job challenges, and Michelle was curious about his future. I recall giving Phil a reading that evening. Time seemed to fly by. The next thing I knew, Michelle was helping me wash the dishes. They were getting ready to leave.

"Thanks, Dayle, for the delicious dinner. We had a wonderful time. I have to get home a little early tonight because I'm scheduled to fly tomorrow."

"No problem. I hope to see the two of you soon." Blythe and I walked Michelle and Phil to the car.

April 28, 1988. I was driving my car to Zippy's, a local restaurant in the Islands. I turned on the radio and listened to my favorite station, KSSK. All of a sudden I heard, "Aloha Airlines Flight 243 is having trouble from Hilo to Honolulu." The reporter seemed somewhat shaken. I listened intently.

My Psychic powers kicked in: I began to space out. I started mumbling to myself, "Michelle . . . she's on that flight; I know she's on that flight."

Suddenly, I was mentally there; I was on Flight 243 with Michelle! I felt cold; I could see the sky above me. What happened? Was there a bomb? People were silent, yet scared. There was blood all around. I frantically searched my mind's eye for Michelle. Where was she? I couldn't find her. My eyes glanced downward. There she was, lying on the floor. I saw a man holding her down so she wouldn't become airborne. Michelle seemed bruised, but she was alive.

I forced my mind to go further. I searched the plane, but I couldn't see the pilot. How was the plane flying? Were all these people dead? Was I dreaming? I forced my mind to go even further. I could see the faces of the passengers; they were in shock. I glanced around. There was another flight attendant pressed to the floor of the plane. I glanced back at Michelle. Somehow I knew she would be all right. A *knowing* feeling came over me; I knew the plane would land safely.

Then, once again, my mind and my body became one. I was concentrating on the road again, rushing toward home to confirm what I saw. When I got there, I raced into my house, picked up the phone and dialed Phil's number rapidly. The phone rang and rang. Phil finally answered.

"Phil, this is Dayle. Did you hear about Aloha Airlines, Flight 243? Is it safe? Michelle is on that plane, isn't she?" I didn't give Phil a chance to answer. I kept rambling on.

"Dayle, calm down," Phil said. "The plane is safe. It just landed in Kahului, Maui. Yes, Michelle is on the plane. She's fine, just a little bit bruised. I just heard from her." Phil sounded calm but shaken.

"Thank God!" I replied. "I know you'll have your hands full, but please keep me informed," I said.

"Thanks for calling. Watch the news reports. They should give you a lot more information."

I glanced at Blythe. He was glued to the television.

The vision was over but the nightmare had just begun.

For just a moment in time I had been there with Michelle. This is called *remote viewing*. Physically, I was in one place; mentally, I was in another place.

I flashed on what the fortune teller had told me three months ago and started to analyze what she had said. She had spoken of a death in the family; shortly thereafter, Blythe's grandmother had died. She had said the plane was over water, maybe the Outer Islands. That it was. She saw it going down and that I would be saved.

But it wasn't *me* the event was happening to; it was my friend Michelle. What the fortune teller saw was wrong. Yet, at the same time, she was right. She was able to see the vision through my eyes. Part of me was to experience this event firsthand.

Two weeks later. After the commotion, I met with Michelle for lunch. I embraced her. "Michelle," I said, "thank God you're alive.

Do you mind if I hold your watch? I want to experience what you went through. I want to look into your future."

I held Michelle's watch intently. Surprisingly, I experienced her feelings while she was flying. I felt her trauma and her pain. Mystically, I was projected into Michelle's future.

I saw fame around her. I saw her receiving award after award. I envisioned a movie being made in regards to Aloha Airlines. I saw her going to Washington, D.C., to receive awards for bravery. Fame was her lot. I was sweating throughout this whole ordeal. As I finished her reading, I turned to her and said, "There's no more danger. You're safe. I can't believe how brave you were. You should be very proud of yourself; you saved many lives."

Michelle responded, "That's the problem. I don't feel I did enough."

"Michelle, you did more than enough, more than any one person could do under those circumstances," I said. She had a look of sadness on her face. "What's wrong?" I asked.

"Dayle, it's my father, even though he has passed on. When he was my age, he was a pilot in Vietnam. At age thirty-five he was honored with three Purple Hearts, a Silver Star, and the Distinguished Flying Cross. He was a very brave man. I can't help but wonder, if he were alive today, would he be proud of me?" Tears ran down her cheeks as she told me this story. "I just can't help but think I could have done more to help those people."

I said, "Michelle, someday you'll realize just how important you were. Not only did you help save lives, but you watched over your people until you felt they were well enough to leave the hospital. The most important thing you must remember is that you're alive for a reason. It's up to you to try to find out why you are here and what your true destiny is.

"That flight was a death flight. There was no logical reason why anyone lived. Let's go over it together—maybe then you'll realize just how much you contributed to the world, not to mention the fact that you're a part of history. Tell me in your own words what you saw and what really happened. I'll follow along with you mentally."

Michelle began:

"Capt. Robert Schornstheimer was the pilot. Second in command was Mimi Tompkins. Then there was C.B. Lancing, a wonderful flight attendant. She had flown for Aloha ever since it began. C.B. loved her job. She was a mother to all us girls, always kept us in line. Then there was Jane Sato Tomita, another flight attendant. We were close to her as well.

"We were on our way from Hilo to Honolulu, and everything seemed quite normal. I was stationed in the back of the plane. C.B. was in the front along with Jane.

"There were eighty-nine passengers and five crew members aboard. We were about ten minutes into the flight and approximately twenty-seven minutes from Honolulu. A loud backfire sound came out of nowhere. I flew up to the ceiling of the cabin and landed in the aisle. Debris and sections of the aircraft were whipping passengers. The wind was deafening. The wind had a strength five times greater than a hurricane. My back was to the hole of the aircraft. I finally got up and crawled around."

"The plane seemed to be flying by itself. I really didn't know if the captain was flying the plane or not, because I couldn't make it to the cockpit. When we reached a lower altitude, I was able to get up off the floor. I made my way toward the front of the plane. The wind was horrendous. I could barely move."

I was listening intently to every word Michelle was saying. I was trying to find some hidden meanings. Maybe I was trying to fill in the parts that she could no longer remember.

Michelle continued as if she were in a trance. "I saw arms dangling in midair, hair flying all over the place. There was blood all over. Then I spotted Jane; she was on the floor, helpless. I reached down to her and held her in my arms. 'Don't worry, Jane; we're going to land soon. Hang in there, please hang in there,' I said. I demanded that one of the passengers hold on to her. I asked him to put his weight on her so she wouldn't become airborne."

Michelle shuddered. "Dayle, it was terrible. The whole thing was terrible," she said. "I couldn't make my way to the cockpit. I didn't know what was going on. I decided to get the life jackets ready just in case we landed in the water. The rest of the time I spent helping the passengers put on their life jackets.

"The plane seemed to be turning. It looked as if we were headed for Maui. That's all I remember, Dayle, until the plane landed safely in Maui." Michelle's voice faded as she spoke her last words to me.

"Michelle, I know that you were saved for a reason, as well as every passenger on that plane," I said.

Weeks later, Blythe and I watched the news coverage very intently. We learned that Capt. Schornstheimer and Ms. Tompkins had had their hands full in the cockpit. They had no communication to the tower. The noise was too loud for a conversation.

"Mayday, Mayday, this is Flight 243, Aloha Airlines. Emergency. Mayday. We are experiencing rapid decompression." After extreme effort Ms. Tompkins was able to communicate with the captain *only* through hand signals. Several attempts later, the control tower in Maui finally received the message.

There, everyone sprang into action. The hospitals were on alert. The fire engines were ready to go. Meanwhile, in the cockpit, the pilots had no idea if the landing gear had come down. It had, and the Maui control tower guided the plane all the way to a safe landing. Capt. Robert Schornstheimer and Mimi Tompkins had gone beyond their line of duty, and they had saved the lives of all passengers.

In actuality, everyone could have died in two different instances. The first was when the top ripped off the plane; all on board could have been sucked out. The second was while the plane was landing; it could have broken into a million pieces and caught on fire. The plane landed safely and all were saved, thanks to Capt. Schornstheimer and Ms. Tompkins.

Even though the plane was on the ground, Michelle wasn't through yet. She helped evacuate the plane and made sure everyone was safe. The only fatality was C.B. Lancing. For weeks on end, Michelle visited each one of her passengers until they all were nursed back to health.

I thought to myself, this very brave young lady was so fragile and dear, yet she had the courage of twenty men. Along with the captain and copilot, she was able to break through the barriers of fate and time and to help save many lives.

I searched my mind. Why was this flight saved? By right it was a death flight. How could this plane stay airborne? The whole top of the plane had ripped off in flight. How was this plane flying? They call it the *Miracle Landing of Flight 243*.

Why were they saved? I'll tell you why! It was because the pilot and copilot, as well as the flight attendants, were more concerned for their passengers than they were for themselves. Their bravery was beyond that of most human beings.

As for Michelle, I knew her personally, and she couldn't help but care for everyone on that plane. She worked endlessly.

As I had predicted, months later Michelle and the rest of the crew of Flight 243 received awards from Washington, D.C. A movie was made. The crew of Flight 243 became known nationally and internationally.

What I learned from this situation is that the vision of a Psychic is not always correct. Sometimes it's like a puzzle that has to be pieced together inch by inch. There are many times when Psychics save people's lives. Many times predictions help guide people along the way.

Sometimes pieces of a puzzle will come into play months or even years later, in a totally unexpected way. It may even seem like a mere coincidence, but I have to wonder just how many "coincidences" have to occur before people realize that life is much more purposeful than we generally suspect.

About one year later, a gentleman came to me for a reading. In that reading he disclosed he had been on Flight 243. He mentioned that he held Michelle down so she wouldn't become airborne. Michelle never knew the person who helped save her life. I gave the gentleman her phone number. The circle was complete.

Michelle Honda and I still talk now and then. I hope Michelle found out that in a time of crisis she was more than brave. I know her father would have been very proud of her, for he is watching from above.

Just a special note to Michelle, one of my dearest friends:
May you always be guided, for surely God walks with you on each and every journey that you take.

I am so proud to have known such a brave, wonderful, warm-hearted person such as you. You were surely saved for a reason. Someday you will know that reason.

All my love and the deepest respect, Michelle. You will never know how many lives you have changed. You gave from the heart. It's called **the Aloha Spirit.**

All the events that occurred in this chapter are true. And I believe everything happens in our lives for a reason.

CHAPTER 4

GALAXY AIRLINES FLIGHT 203

The Aloha Airlines jet was not the first, nor the last, whose flight path had crossed my mind.

Reno Gazette Journal, December 31, 1983:

> **The Touch**
> "I pick up a major plane disaster in Reno—soon.
> Within 10 years, Reno will be a big city—a major city.
> The Mayor will go far. He's an honest man.
> New industry moving in . . . computer companies, electronics companies."
> Along with her vision of the mayor's future, Schear began to make predictions for the city. Her forecast of more direct flights into Reno seemed to call up a disturbing image. *"I do pick up a major plane disaster in Reno,"* she said. "It's close. Maybe 1984, maybe sooner. I don't know exactly when, but soon."

Reno Gazette Journal, January 21, 1985:

> **63 Die in Fiery Reno Air Crash**
> A charter airplane en route to Minneapolis from Reno crashed "in a ball of fire" at 1:04 a.m. today on south Virginia Street in

28

the Meadowood area, reportedly killing between 63 and 66 people in the city's first major air disaster. . . .

Predictions are not my forte. Each year newspapers scramble to find local Psychics to peer into the future. Psychics and predictions are synonymous with apple pie and coffee.

I recall making these predictions in the latter part of December 1983. I thought to myself, what a strange thing to say, that there will be a major plane crash in Reno. I'd better be careful. There are so many people out there who believe in what I say. I don't want to scare anyone. Besides, Reno has never had a major plane disaster.

Then it happened. On January 21, 1985, Galaxy Airlines Flight 203 crashed shortly after takeoff. It was exactly thirteen months later, just as I foretold. I was one month off. Out of seventy-one souls aboard, only one survived the crash.

Galaxy Airlines Flight 203 had arrived from Seattle via Oakland about three hours behind schedule. The plane still had to return to Seattle, en route to Minneapolis. The Electra jet was serviced around midnight, the passengers boarded, and the engines started just a few minutes before 1:00 a.m.

According to the Federal Aviation Administration's report on the crash, shortly after the plane took off, there was a mysterious thump. A forceful, steady vibration shook the plane. Flight 203's black box recorded the final desperate moments in the cockpit.

"Tell'em we've got a heavy vibration," the captain said.

"Pull up! Pull up!" yelled the flight engineer.

The captain called for full power.

Six seconds later the airplane struck the ground in a shallow descent and burst into flames. Bits and pieces of body parts lay all over the street. My prediction had come to pass. A prediction such as this one has no rhyme nor reason. I had been able to see thirteen months into the future.

I watched the news closely: my eyes were glued to the television set, taking in all the gory details. Of the seventy-one souls aboard that flight, all but three died in the crash. The three were Robert Miggins, 45; George Lamson, Sr., 41; and Lamson's son, George Jr., 17. Of these three survivors, only one recovered from his injuries and lived.

Robert Miggins was taken to Nevada Memorial Hospital, reportedly conscious and with burns over ninety percent of his body. His struggle for life ended shortly thereafter.

George Lamson, Sr., had multiple skull and facial fractures; his lungs were seared and he had burns over fifteen percent of his body. He drifted in and out of consciousness and died eight days later.

George Lamson, Jr., who had been sitting next to his father on the plane, was the *only one* of the seventy-one passengers to walk away from the crash and live. I can't help but wonder *why* he was saved.

The survivor tells it all: "As the plane took off," he said, "passengers were in high spirits, but some were drunk and ignored the safety instructions of a stewardess."

Flight 203 had given him a "scary feeling" even before the plane plowed into the ground near U.S. 395.

"Although the takeoff was smooth," Lamson said, "the plane soon ran into what seemed to be turbulence, which bounced the craft up and down. Everybody else was just laughing in the airplane and saying, 'Oh, it's nothing.' But then we started going down. All I saw was sky out of the window; then, all of a sudden, I saw that the ground was coming closer. Then the pilot said, 'We're coming down!' And then we crashed."

As the other passengers screamed with fright, Lamson said, "I brought my legs up and I covered up my head with my hands. I was sitting right by the wall, so I kicked the wall while we hit the ground. I was in my seat with my seat belt on, sliding through all this fire and debris. Something was burning me on the face; I don't know what it was . . . I just got out of there as soon as possible.

"Then I realized I was outside and I tried to get out. I ripped off my seat belt and ran. I was waving my hands and screaming that I was alive and needed someone to help me. The people who found me were just as surprised as I was." Lamson had been miraculously tossed clear of the wreckage.

He escaped with a forehead laceration and burns to his face, hands and forearms in the crash. He said, "I just feel I was in the right place at the right time. That's how I survived."

Another spooky thing happened that night. Galaxy airlines was a charter flight for Caesar's Tahoe. Carl Jackson was one of the drivers of the Nevada Golden Tour buses that took a number of the doomed passengers to Reno Cannon International Airport from Caesar's Tahoe. For some unknown reason, the buses, instead of being allowed to remain as usual by the plane while the passengers boarded, were told to go back to the parking lot. Jackson said he believed it was because the plane had to be tidied up after dropping off some Super Bowl travelers, whom he was to bus back to Caesar's.

Normally, he would have waited for his initial passengers to board their plane. By the time he would have been driving back toward Carson City on South Virginia Street, the plane would have been taking off directly overhead.

It was at a spot on the edge of South Virginia Street where the big charter plane crashed in a ball of fire. As Jackson figures it, if he had followed his usual routine after dropping the load of passengers at the airport, he might have been there on South Virginia Street at that time. "The timing scares me," he says. "We were in Carson City, but ordinarily we would have been at about where the plane crashed."

Jackson, who drove about twenty-five of the people to the plane, and Dan O'Rourke, who drove a similar number, have talked about the accident and both "feel guilt," Jackson said.

"Dan said, 'If only I had had a flat tire, maybe it wouldn't have happened.'" "But," Jackson said, "It wouldn't have made any difference. That plane was waiting for them."

The mysteries of fate are not new to Jackson. There was another plane at another time: in 1978, a PSA jet and a small private plane collided in the air over San Diego, killing everyone in both aircraft.

Jackson, who was living in Los Angeles then, had been booked on the flight to San Diego. At the last moment he was unexpectedly called to Seattle and didn't take the PSA flight.

Another strange story to tell. The same Galaxy Airlines plane that crashed in Reno had been chartered before by former presidential candidate Jesse Jackson.

The pilot of the aircraft, Al Heasley, had flown Jackson often during the campaign, and the stewardesses who died in the Reno crash had served with Heasley during many of those flights, Jackson said in an interview.

The candidate stopped using the Galaxy Airlines charter plane following a turbulent, five-hour flight from Dallas to Washington. He was accompanied by about sixty campaign aides, Secret Service agents and reporters. During the flight the plane was buffeted by bad weather, causing some passengers to scream and sob as personal belongings and television equipment flew about the cabin.

"My anxiety level hit the breaking point," Jackson said after the flight. "It was just too much for me."

After the flight, Jackson asked federal authorities to inspect the plane, and both company officials and Federal Aviation Administration inspectors said that they found nothing wrong.

According to the F.A.A., the cause of the crash of Galaxy Airlines was an open access door about the size of a sheet of paper. The door, which covered the air-start hose attach fitting, had been left open by the ground crew. Also, the F.A.A. felt that pilot error could not be ruled out.

Galaxy Airlines Flight 203 was the most devastating crash in the history of Reno.

The Way I See It

We hear of these stories all the time: Several Die in Plane Crash. Why are the few who survive meant to live? I have a theory that the survivors of the world are left here on this planet to help others. For some unknown reason they are given a second chance. It's up to them to find their true destinies.

I can't help but wonder why I couldn't have changed this event, if I can see into the future. After all my years of experience, I now know the answer.

There are major events in this world that are predestined. These are the events that cannot be changed, such as the assassinations of John F. Kennedy and Bobby Kennedy. When a major event is about to occur, no one on this earth can alter it or change it in any way that we know of at this time. As the years progress, this theory may change.

However, we do have free-will choices in our lives to change certain things. I would say we can change or alter about eighty percent of what may be our free-will choices. The other twenty percent cannot be altered.

Example: In the movie, *The Dead Zone* by Stephen King, Christopher Walken portrays a Psychic who has visions while holding a young boy. He sees the child drowning in a lake during an ice hockey practice with his friends. Walken tries to alter the boy's future. He tells the father about the accident that will occur. The father refuses to believe the Psychic and orders the boy to play ice hockey anyway. The boy refuses. Later that afternoon the ice breaks and three children die. The boy who refused to play ice hockey, the same boy who was warned by the Psychic, lived. The event of the children drowning still occurred. However, the boy's future was altered and his life was saved.

So, as you can see in this tiny example of life, one can sometimes alter a person's future. The whole point behind Steven King's movie *The Dead Zone* is whether *there is a probability of altering the future.*

How do we know the difference? We don't. All we can do is try. When a mother has a vision of her child in danger, it's up to the mother to react, to try to do something about it. The most important factor is not to ignore what one feels or sees. If something inside you says, "Don't take that plane," listen to that voice within. Don't slough it off as some crazy vision. Reacting just may save your life.

In conclusion, George Lamson, Jr., the seventeen-year-old survivor of a plane crash, had a mighty story to tell, but what he must truly learn from all this is that he survived for a reason. Someday George Lamson, Jr., may play a role in this world. Someday he may save hundreds of other people's lives.

There is a reason we live.
There is a reason we die.
There is a reason some survive.
For every action there is a reaction.
Every thought we put out in this world
Affects hundreds of other people.
There is a purpose to all mankind.
Maybe, just maybe, George Lamson, Jr.
Will save your life someday.

CHAPTER 5

COME FLY WITH ME

Reno Airport, 1983. I was en route to Burbank, California, via Pacific Southwest Airlines to meet with my mentor, Peter Hurkos. I handed the flight attendant my ticket. She smiled and said, "Have a good flight." I touched the airplane, my usual procedure before boarding. I had a feeling something was wrong. I searched my mind to try to find the answer. The landing gear! There was something wrong with the landing gear.

I turned around nervously, looking for the pilot. I had to speak with the pilot. I glanced in the cockpit; he wasn't there, so I went searching for him. There he was, playing the slot machines in the Reno airport, killing time.

"Excuse me," I said. "Are you the pilot of this plane?"

"Yes," he replied, as he pulled the handle of the slot machine.

"I know this is going to sound strange, but I think there's something wrong with your landing gear."

He continued playing. "The landing gear is fine. It's the indicator light that's malfunctioning. We're waiting for the part to come in." He paused momentarily and looked up. "How did you know?"

"I'm a Psychic. Whenever I board a plane I always touch it to make sure the flight will go smoothly. When I touched this plane, I felt as though we weren't going to land."

"I believe in Psychics," he said. "Young lady, you were right, but we're aware of the problem. Rest assured the flight will be smooth. We'll land safely. Can I walk you back to the plane? After I check everything out, we'll take off."

My mind was at peace. We landed in Burbank within forty minutes.

Ever since I can remember, flying makes me somewhat uneasy. Since I'm not in control of the situation, I always panic before a flight. I've noticed that the more I panic, the more mechanical things go wrong with the plane. I've tried everything to calm myself down, but nothing has worked so far.

Flying with a Psychic can be an adventure. Upon recognizing me, a flight attendant would shout out, "I guess this plane is perfectly safe; we have a Psychic flying with us!" This is a true statement to some extent. If I sense danger, I'm out of there. If not, the flight will be perfectly safe.

Every Psychic has a Psychic. On most occasions I usually ask one of my Psychic friends to check out my flight for me. At times I have to rely on myself for the answers. This is when my life becomes difficult. As long as I have a few drinks and remain calm throughout the trip, all will be fine. Somehow I always know how the plane trip is going to turn out.

Example: When Blythe and I were to fly back to Hawaii from Alaska, I developed a very uneasy feeling about the trip. I felt something was wrong, but I couldn't put my finger on what. I didn't want to go. When we were seated on the plane, I asked him to turn my watch back so I would be on Hawaii time. Several minutes passed. For some reason the hands of my watch would not budge.

Blythe finally said, "Dayle, something's wrong with your watch. I can't turn the watch back. Don't worry, I'll fix it when we land."

"I don't think so, Blythe!"

"What do you mean?" he said.

"I've learned from experience that when my watch refuses to go forward or backward in time, it's a sign that we're not going anywhere. This plane will turn around."

Blythe stared at me and asked, "Do you feel any danger?"

"No," I replied.

About an hour into the flight, everything seemed calm, but I couldn't shake the feeling I was having. Sure enough, the pilot announced over the loudspeaker that he was turning the plane around. Because of manifold problems, we were headed back to Alaska.

The plane landed safely. All passengers were asked to remain seated. Blythe looked at me, I at him, and off we went. We decided to stay in Anchorage for a little while longer. I figured I was meant to stay for a reason. It just so happened there were several people who had not been able to see me for consultations earlier, and when they found out I was in town for an extra few days, they were grateful.

Another time, I was on my way to Honolulu to meet with Blythe. Two hours into the flight the pilot asked over the loudspeaker, "Is there a doctor on the plane?" There was. A flight attendant took the doctor to a man who had just passed out, apparently from a heart attack. The doctor was trying to revive him.

An hour passed. I left my seat to check out the situation. I watched the doctor work on his patient and wondered to myself why he was continuing to work on this man. The man was dead!

Shortly thereafter, the pilot's voice came on over the loudspeaker. "Sorry, folks, one of our passengers has passed away. We are considering turning the plane around and going back to San Francisco." Twenty minutes passed. The pilot decided to continue on course to Hawaii. Just before landing, the pilot asked all passengers to say a prayer. A eulogy was also given. What a strange flight.

Another instance in regards to travel involved something that happens to all of us, losing one's luggage!

Blythe and I were in Newark, New Jersey, preparing for our return trip to Los Angeles. I asked Blythe to repack our luggage, for I knew it would be lost or stolen en route. In our luggage were several family photos that were irreplaceable and precious to me. When I was a child living in Lakewood, New Jersey, our house burned down and there were hardly any photos left of our family. I had flown 2,500 miles to retrieve these photos from my relatives and I wasn't about to lose them. Blythe decided to hand carry the pictures.

When we arrived in L.A., we both left the airport to get our rental car. When we returned to the baggage area, two of our bags were still circling the carousel. The rest of our luggage was lost. Till this day United Airlines has never recovered our luggage. Fortunately, because I knew I was going to lose my luggage, I prevented my pictures from being lost.

There is order to my madness when I fly. One trip we took from Newark to Reno, via San Francisco, was unique in itself. I was anxious to make it home; I had spent two long weeks working on a murder case in New York. Blythe and I boarded United Airlines once again homeward bound.

I felt good about this flight. I rested my eyes. All at once I could see mechanics all over the plane. When I opened my eyes, there they were. The pilot announced we would be delayed for a while, due to mechanical problems. I projected myself mentally into the future. I could see that if we stayed on the plane I would miss my connecting flight to Reno, which would cause at least a six-hour delay. I hate delays. I said to Blythe, "Come on, we're getting out of here." We quickly left the plane. I had a lot of explaining to do. United let us go, and we left on another airline. Several hours later I checked the United flight and found out the plane was indeed several hours late. I would have missed my connecting flight to Reno.

I had another adventure while traveling with a girlfriend on my way to San Francisco. This happened to be a very traumatic time for me. I was leaving Hawaii on my way to Lake Tahoe; it was to be a permanent move, and I was hesitant. Part of me did not want to leave, the other part of me did. As soon as I set foot on the plane, I felt very uneasy about the flight. Suddenly, I picked up my traveling case and said, "I'm getting out of here!" My girlfriend followed. When we reached the door, the flight attendant stopped us.

"Why are you leaving, Ms. Schear?" she asked.

"I don't know. I don't feel very good about this flight," I replied.

"Don't worry. There's nothing to worry about, I assure you."

This was one of the very few times I listened. I took my seat next to my friend, still somewhat uneasy. I found out later that I had been picking up, through telepathy, the flight attendants' feelings.

The flight attendants did not want to be on this flight. They were working back-to-back shifts and their attitudes were pouring into my soul. I was reading their minds and I felt uneasy. However, once again the plane did land safely.

My latest adventure occurred while I was writing this book, *The Psychic Within*. We boarded United Airlines, once again on our way to San Francisco. The flight was smooth and everything was going well. Blythe and I sat upstairs in the huge, 747 stretch plane. I was settling in when one of the stewards announced that our upstairs restroom was broken. No big thing, I thought; I'll get my exercise for the day by walking up and down the stairs.

About two hours into the flight, I made my rounds and introduced myself to the flight attendants. The fact that I was on board created quite a bit of chatter among them. One of the flight attendants asked about my book, *Dare To Be Different*. The next thing I knew, they were buying my book and asking for my autograph. I was delighted.

When I took my seat again, I started drifting into a deep sleep. Something awoke me, but I can't remember what. I literally jumped out of my seat. For no apparent reason I walked down the stairs towards the restrooms. Then I saw a man stretched out on the floor with a doctor attending him. I sat on the stairs and focused in on the gentleman, who was in his late thirties, trying to figure out what was wrong with him. His eyes were wide open, staring at the ceiling.

Suddenly, I saw him leave his body. He was having an *out-of-body experience,* which is the soul leaving the physical body. I was puzzled. I thought this only happened when one is dying. The astral body came towards me. This frightened me. I shouted to it in my mind, "Go back, go back in your body! You're not dead." I was paralyzed, unable to speak aloud. When I finally regained my voice, I asked the flight attendants to give the man some orange juice. "He's having a low-blood-sugar attack!" I yelled. Without delay they reacted, and within moments the man's color came back. The attendants found out the man hadn't eaten for hours. They thanked me.

Later into the flight I mentioned to the flight attendants that I was writing a chapter all about flying in my new book, *The Psychic Within*. They smiled and said, "We can't wait to read the part about this flight!"

As I went upstairs to tell Blythe what had happened, I shook my head and wondered why I never could get a normal flight. Why did these things always happen to me? I related the whole story to Blythe. "But, Blythe, there's one thing I don't understand." I asked, "Why was the man leaving his body when he wasn't dead?"

Blythe explained, "Apparently, we have out-of-body experiences not only when we die, but sometimes when the body goes into shock, or when we're sleeping. The man's astral body was coming toward you because you were familiar to him. He came to you for help."

"What do you mean 'familiar to him'? He never met me," I said.

Blythe replied, "No, Dayle, I meant you were on the same vibrational frequency as him. You know, just like when you tune into someone, the man tuned into you for help."

"I understand now. I guess we can always learn something new," I said. "Blythe, just once I would like to have a normal flight, like everyone else."

He smiled. "Oh, would you?"

The rest of the flight was smooth sailing.

Understanding Psychics When They Fly

Psychics are very sensitive people. We tend to sense danger way before most people. We naturally check out flights, especially if we are flying on them. Psychics will not put themselves into a dangerous situation.

I trained with Peter Hurkos, the greatest Psychic of the century. Peter would not only touch a plane to see if it would land safely, but he would also touch a passenger and peer into that person's future to make sure everything would be fine. Peter always taught me that if you look at a plane or touch a plane and see blackness or a void in your mind's eye, do not board the plane, for surely it will crash.

Over the years I developed my own method. I will mentally trace my route from the time I board the plane till the time I arrive. If I can't see myself arriving at a certain destination, I know I'm in trouble.

Psychics pick up on disasters easily. Again, we are dealing with telepathy, the reading of the mind. When someone is hurt or injured, their emotional state is at a peak. Thoughts travel fast. Since a Psychic is a natural receiver, it's easy for a Psychic to pick up the telepathic information. ESP is based on feelings and emotions, and an emotion or feeling is easy to pick up on.

There are many Psychics who pick up on impending airplane crashes. There is no explanation for this whatsoever. Most information a Psychic uses is based on telepathy. But picking up a plane crash several weeks before it happens is not telepathy. This falls into another category.

This is *clairvoyance,* or seeing an event before it happens. Clairvoyance is the ability to perceive things not in sight and without any other knowledge of the event.

Example: A Psychic sees a plane crashing two weeks from now in L.A. The Psychic can't read the mind of a person to find out this information, so we can rule out telepathy. When all reasoning and logic are ruled out, all that remains is clairvoyance, seeing the future.

Certain events in our lives are meant to be. Some people call these events "destiny." Our lives are somewhat predestined. Yet, at the same time, we have free-will choice. It's hard to distinguish the difference between destiny—what is meant to be—and free-will choice. Sometimes one has to wait till the outcome occurs before one can determine the difference.

Example: A man boards an airplane. The plane crashes. Everyone dies, except that particular man. It was his destiny to live.

The next man boards a plane. The plane crashes; he dies. That was his destiny.

Now we have a third man who, before he flies, decides to visit a Psychic. The Psychic tells him, "I see danger around a flight that you are going to take. If I were you, I would take another flight."

This is where free-will choice comes in. It's up to the man to decide whether to take the flight or not. This particular man chooses not to fly that day. He later finds out that his plane crashed and all aboard perished. Now, by using his free will and not flying that day, was that his destiny? Was he meant to visit with the Psychic so she could forewarn him of the impending disaster? Or was it just free-will choice that saved his life? *Who can say?*

The moral of this story is, you're safe if you fly with a Psychic. Take a Psychic along with you to insure your flight. If by chance your Psychic decides to leave the plane before it takes off, the best advice I can give you is to follow your Psychic wherever he or she goes!

CHAPTER 6

THE *ACHILLE LAURO* INCIDENT

October 1985. It was late at night; I was lying in bed. It seemed I was in a dream state; not yet awake, nor fully asleep. I recall dreaming. Ah! I remember the dream well.

I woke up out of sound sleep screaming. I reached for my husband Blythe, as if he could somehow hold me and make things better. I gasped for air.

Blythe awoke. "What's wrong?" he asked.

"I was dreaming. It was horrible!" I cried.

"What was the dream about?"

"I was on a cruise ship in the middle of the ocean. There was no way off the ship; I was stuck. There were two or three men keeping watch over me. Suddenly, I broke away. I tried to get off the ship, but every exit was blocked. The men had guns."

"Was there anyone else on the ship?" Blythe asked.

"Yes, there were a lot of people. I was running fast. I wanted to try to make my way off the ship. I noticed there were people on the floor. I don't understand what this means."

"We'll try to make sense of it in the morning. Go back to sleep; you're safe now," he said.

"Safe," I thought to myself. "Maybe Blythe is right." I drifted off to sleep.

The same dream recurred, night after night. The dream grew more intense. I was trapped on a cruise ship; I couldn't get off. Suddenly, the dream or vision that lured me into this plot reminded me of a movie.

I recall there were two or three men holding me at bay. They were armed. No matter how hard I tried to leave, every exit was blocked. I began to see the men. They wore bandannas on their heads. They spoke with an accent. I didn't recognize who they were.

Blythe suggested I search my mind, "Can you see the colors of the ship? Do you recognize anyone on board?"

"I don't know, Blythe. All I know is I'm frightened. Maybe I'm seeing the future?" We tried to make sense of it; however, there wasn't any sense to be made of this incident.

But there was something unusual about this. I had just appeared on an American-Hawaii Cruise Ship a little over a week before. Maybe someone was going to sabotage the ship. Who could I call; who would believe me? I had to let this go for a while and wait to see what would happen.

One Week Later. We were watching the news on television. Instantaneously, the ship in my dreams was now live on television! We watched in awe. A ship in the middle of the ocean had been captured. The name of the ship was the *Achille Lauro.*

News bulletin, October 1985. "The ship was off the coast of Egypt. Most of the passengers on the Italian cruise ship *Achille Lauro* were on a day trip to see the pyramids. The few remaining passengers on board the ship were having lunch in the ship's dining room. Suddenly, shots were heard outside. Gunmen charged in, spraying the room with bullets. The passengers fell to the floor."

The 53-hour ordeal had begun. Before it was over, sixty-nine-year-old, wheelchair-dependent passenger Leon Klinghoffer would be murdered. His body would be thrown overboard.

This was my dream. Why was this happening? I didn't know any of these people. This was not a coincidence; this was real. I couldn't make sense of it, but I knew someday the pieces would fit. Fit they did! At the time this was happening, I never understood why I was dreaming of this ship, nor why I felt what the passengers were going through.

I do now! About four years later, in October of 1989, Blythe and I were about to embark on my first trip back to New Jersey, the place where I was born. I was in the midst of gathering information for my first book, *Dare to Be Different!* I was about to visit my relatives, whom I hadn't seen for well over twenty years.

This was a happy occasion for me. One of my first stops was the home of my cousin David Glyn and his family. David and I grew up together. We hadn't seen each other for what seemed like eternity. My mother used to always take me to David's house to play as a child. David was very special in my life; I always looked up to him. There was something very unique about him. He was shy as a child, yet confident. He was a leader graced with an extreme amount of spirituality, a knowing sense of right and wrong. It seemed fitting that he would grow up to be a lawyer, and a darn good one at that.

We were about to meet after almost twenty years. As I opened the car door, there they were, all eight of them. Yes, eight of them, including David and his wife Rachel. They invited Blythe and me into their home. David and I talked for hours on end, trying to catch up on the past.

The conversation switched gears. I asked David if he could tell me where our grandmother was buried. I wanted to put flowers on her grave. David looked at me in amazement. "You mean you don't know where Grandma is buried? I mean, no one told you?"

"No," I replied.

"Grandma is buried in the same family plot where the Klinghoffers are."

"Klinghoffers! You mean that man who was shot on the *Achille Lauro*?"

"Yes," David replied. "Dayle, that's our first cousin Marilyn and her husband Leon Klinghoffer."

"Whoa!" I couldn't believe what I was hearing.

"What's the matter? You mean you didn't know about the Klinghoffers?" David sounded surprised.

"David, I knew indirectly." I proceeded to explain about my dreams. David was now the one who was quite amazed.

"David, would you mind explaining to me what happened? Can you tell me everything you know about the Klinghoffers?" I was about to put together the pieces of a puzzle.

"Sit down, Dayle and Blythe. I have a story to tell you. It all started when we were kids. I don't think you would remember Marilyn and Leon very well. On occasion we would all meet at family gatherings. They were well off. They purchased a cemetery plot for the whole Glyn family, including Grandma. That's why she's buried next to my dad and Leon Klinghoffer."

"David, that's all very interesting; I don't remember these people. I can't figure out why I would have dreamt about the boat and Leon Klinghoffer. There must be some sort of a telepathic bond that I have with my family," I said. "Anyway, explain to me about the ship and exactly what happened. Maybe I can piece some of the information together."

"Dayle, sit back; I need to gather my thoughts." David remained in heavy contemplation. When he spoke, his voice trembled with anger.

He shouted, "Leon was a Jew! That's why they killed him! It's as simple as that." His eyes filled with tears, but he continued the conversation.

"Wait a minute, Dayle. I have a scrapbook regarding this incident. Let's go through the newspaper articles together." I was excited!

David read aloud from the clippings. This was the story that emerged:

October 1985. Marilyn Klinghoffer was celebrating her fifty-ninth birthday with her husband Leon and friends. They were setting sail aboard the *Achille Lauro,* an Italian cruise ship. The cruise was Marilyn's birthday present. Their itinerary included an eleven-day cruise from Genoa to Naples, Alexandria, Port Said, Ashdod Limassol, Rhodes, Capri, and back to Genoa.

Leon Klinghoffer was sixty-nine years old. He had suffered a stroke that left him partially paralyzed. Marilyn had terminal cancer. This would be the last cruise they would take together. The ship set course for Naples, Syracuse and Alexandria. Most of the passengers went ashore at Alexandria; more than 650 of the 748 passengers disembarked to see the Pyramids. Leon Klinghoffer wasn't able to make the trip that would have saved his life.

Hijackers took over the ship. Gunshots were heard throughout the ship. Gunmen charged in, spraying the dining room with bullets. Passengers headed for the floor. Four terrorists seized the ship. They declared themselves part of the Palestinian Liberation Organization. They wanted to trade Americans and Jews for fifty PLO prisoners. When the terrorists realized they were getting nowhere, they decided to kill one of the passengers to show that they meant business. The terrorists collected all the passports. When they realized that Leon Klinghoffer was an American and a Jew; he was the first to go. Klinghoffer became a patsy, a martyr.

The terrorists wheeled Klinghoffer to the ship's rail. One of them held his automatic rifle to the American's forehead and opened fire. Klinghoffer's blood spattered over his murderer's pants and shoes. The terrorists walked back into the dining room on A deck, where the passengers from other countries were held. They ordered two of the passengers to go out on deck and throw Klinghoffer and his wheelchair overboard. The terrorists did not want to create panic. When Marilyn Klinghoffer asked where her husband was, the terrorists explained he had suffered a heart seizure and the ship's doctor was looking after him.

At last, though unsuccessful in their efforts to force the release of Palestinians held in Israeli jails, the hijackers did manage to extract a promise of safe passage out of Egypt. They left the *Achille Lauro* after fifty-three hours of terrorism among the passengers and headed for Cairo.

Finally, something went right. The Egyptian airliner carrying the hijackers to freedom was intercepted by U.S. Navy fighters and forced to land in Sicily. Government officials boarded the ship. They asked, "Were there any deaths?"

"Yes!" someone shouted. "I think his name was Klinghoffer."

Marilyn screamed, "You're wrong! You don't know what you're saying!" Marilyn was put under sedation.

The hijackers were arrested. Before Marilyn Klinghoffer returned to New York, she insisted on making a side trip to help identify the four men. There was a trial; the four men were convicted of the crime.

Marilyn's friend Charlotte Spiegel commented to the press: "Leon Klinghoffer was Every Man. He could have been you, he could have been me. And if terrorism is allowed to bloom, his fate could be the fate of everybody."

David sighed. "That's all I know, Dayle." Then he added, "Oh! There is one more thing I remember. Leon's body washed up to shore just before the trial began. Without the body, the terrorists may not have been convicted."

"Must run in the family. Another coincidence?" I said, "Thank you, David, for explaining the situation to me. Somehow I was indirectly a part of this whole ordeal. I still don't know how or why. I guess I have to learn to accept my own gift.

"I can't help but wonder. If the world accepted ESP as a natural occurrence and there were people I could call who would be receptive enough to believe in me . . . maybe, just maybe I could have saved his life." A sadness came over me. "Why won't they listen to us? Why can't people open their minds? Why won't they give us a chance?"

I turned and thanked David and Rachel for sharing this story with me. Blythe and I were ready to go home. "Blythe, maybe someday someone will believe that we as Psychics can help save lives. If you can see the future, sometimes you can change it.

If only they would give us a chance.

CHAPTER 7

THE ART OF SAVING LIVES

"Mama" Ah Cook

January, 1986, Honolulu. It was Sunday evening, as I recall. The phone rang. There was a hysterical woman on the other end of the phone. "Excuse me, Ma'am," I said. "You have to calm down. I don't understand a word you're saying."

"You're Dayle Schear, the Psychic, aren't you?" I could understand her now. "My name is Mrs. Suinn. It's my mother. She wandered away from the nursing home. She's ninety years old. We've been searching for two days, but we can't find her. The police feel there's very little hope. Can you help me?"

"I'll try," I said. "Why don't you come over to my house as soon as possible. I need some of your mother's clothing, and remember to bring some pictures of her with you."

Mrs. Suinn arrived at the house at approximately 9:00 p.m. Blythe and I greeted her and asked her to sit down at my dining room table. With her mother's clothing in one hand and photographs in the other, I began the reading.

My speech became rapid. I was no longer a part of this world; I was in a different reality. My hands touched her clothing. The visions grew more intense.

"She's alive, she's still alive!" I shouted. "She's very close to the nursing home. I see her wandering around the neighborhood. She seems to be walking through a graveyard."

Mrs. Suinn interrupted. "Are you positive about what you are seeing?"

"Yes," I replied. "Why do you question me?"

"Because the police feel that Mama may have gotten on a bus and wandered off. She's done this before, you know. The police also believe she's not in this area because it's a residential area and she would have been spotted. Besides, they claim they've searched the area thoroughly."

I said, " Mrs. Suinn, I don't care what the police think. I know she's close to the nursing home."

"Dayle, I just remembered, . . . there is a graveyard within a block of the nursing home."

"Let's get in our cars and go to the nursing home now!" I shouted. "That way I can feel her presence. Time is of the essence." We jumped in our cars and off we went. We reached the nursing home in record time.

Mrs. Suinn showed us to her mother's room. Within moments my work would begin.

I sat on the bed where Mrs. Cook slept. I held on to some of her clothing as I closed my eyes and cleared my mind of all thoughts. Within moments the visions began. "I see her very close to the nursing home." You could hear a pin drop in the room as I spoke. "We have to look for her now. Within the next twenty-four hours she'll be dead. Let's go!" I shouted.

I was overwhelmed with feelings about this woman. I sensed something unusual about her, yet I couldn't put my finger on it. I could almost hear her shouting for us to find her in my mind. In my heart I felt as though I was searching for my own mother.

When the search began, there were five of us with flashlights in hand, wandering the streets close to the nursing home. We came upon the graveyard. I paused and said, "She's been here. I know she's been here!" We shouted her name. I felt we were close to finding her, but it was very dark. We searched the area till well past midnight with no success. I realized the urgency, but we would have to resume the search in the morning.

I looked straight into the eyes of Cookie Suinn. "You must start your search early in the morning; time is running out. I want you to go up and down each and every street near the nursing home within a one-mile radius. You must leave no stone unturned. I know you *will* find her alive. She seems to be pinned down, looks like a ditch or something. For some reason, if you don't find her tomorrow, it will be too late. Do you understand me?"

"Yes," she replied with anxiety.

The next day the search party started early. Within two hours of the search they found Mrs. Cook lying face down in a ditch behind a church parking lot. She was found within two blocks of the Kaneohe nursing home. Mrs. Cook lay in the hospital for over a week, recovering.

This article appeared in the *Honolulu Star-Bulletin* on Sunday January 19, 1986:

Ben Wood's Hawaii

Cookie Suinn, owner of Cookies's World of Flowers, used the help of Psychic Dayle Schear to locate her ninety-year-old mother, Opunui Ah Cook, who had wandered away from her Kaneohe nursing home. Schear first told Cookie that her mother was alive

> and then told her where she would find the 4-foot-11, 115-pound woman. It was midnight, but both women went to the area. They didn't find her in the darkness, but Mama was found nearby in a ditch the following morning. Opunui, who uses a pacemaker, survived for two days in the ditch, "possibly" doctors said, "because she was used to fasting." Later, as Cookie was cleaning the mud and dirt from her mother's hair and face, the little old lady, in her faint little voice, said, "Ma-a-a-halo," meaning thank you in Hawaiian. How's that for an awwww? . . .

After all the commotion, Mrs. Suinn called me to thank me for helping her find her mother. We got into a deep discussion about her mom. Apparently, when her mother wandered away from the nursing home, she tripped and fell into a ditch. Her dress caught on something; she was unable to get up and barely able to speak.

I kept wondering how a ninety-year-old woman could survive in a ditch with a pacemaker for two days without food or water. I could understand a healthy person surviving, but not a ninety-year-old woman. This was a miracle! Even though this was a miracle in my eyes, I wanted to search further, to know how this miracle could possibly happen.

I found out from Mrs. Suinn that Opunui Ah Cook in her time was considered a healer, a *Kahuna*. The Hawaiian word *Kahuna*, translated into English, means Psychic or healer.

Mrs. Suinn knew this about her mother while she was growing up as a child. She witnessed many unusual happenings in the house, but she was afraid to speak of such things for fear of being called strange. So Mrs. Suinn chose to ignore a lot of unusual occurrences in the home. As she relayed this story about her mother to me, she bent her head in shame. I explained to her there was nothing to be ashamed about. The Hawaiian Islands were built on spirituality. And this, in fact, is probably what saved her mother's life for two days before I came along.

I finally was able to piece together the puzzle. Since her mother was a *Kahuna*, she was able to direct me through telepathy. I acted as a radio receiver. When Mrs. Cook sent out signals that she was in danger, I received her signals. If she were dead, there would be no telepathic transmission from her brain. Since I could feel her and visualize her, I knew she was alive. Even at ninety years of age, she had this incredible power to direct another Psychic to help find her.

When it was all over, I thanked God once again for giving me this gift. With it I was able to help save a life.

About a year later, while viewing television, I watched Opunui Ah Cook celebrate her ninety-first birthday. Tears came to my eyes. It's at times like this I know the gift that was given to me is so very precious for I was chosen to help save a life. Opunui Ah Cook lived to be ninety-five years old.

Phil Simpson

"Dayle warned me of a bad gas leak on my yacht. My mechanic examined it and told me he didn't know what kept me from blowing up."

Phil Simpson is one of my soul mates. I spoke in length about Phil in my first book, *Dare to Be Different!* We traveled the highways and byways together on a spiritual journey that spanned from Lake Tahoe to the Hawaiian Islands. Whenever I was in trouble, Phil was always there by my side. In return, throughout the years I have tried to protect and guide him psychically.

I remember the time Phil asked me to go out on his boat, the *Naughty Lady*, on a hot August day in Lake Tahoe. *The Naughty Lady* is a thirty-six-foot cabin cruiser. Our families were all eager and ready to go. We packed a picnic lunch and off we went, heading toward Emerald Bay in Lake Tahoe, California. We were about an hour into the trip when all of a sudden I turned to Phil and said, "There's a gas leak aboard this boat. The boat isn't safe."

Phil turned to me and asked, "Do you smell the gas?"

"No," I responded. "Phil, I know there's a gas leak. Don't ask me why; I just know. I think you ought to put out your cigarette and we should head back to shore."

Phil turned the boat around and returned to shore. "Please check this boat out for your own safety," I said.

The next day Phil asked the boat mechanic to take a look at the cabin cruiser. Within a week, he reported back to Phil that there was no gas leak. Phil called me at home and relayed the message.

I shouted, "I don't care what this mechanic says; you have a gas leak on board!" Phil demanded that the mechanic look at the boat once again. He did and found nothing again.

Phil and I argued this point. Finally, Phil explained to the mechanic that his Psychic had told him there definitely was a gas leak. The mechanic looked once more. This time he found the leak. He apologized to Phil and stated that if we hadn't found this gas leak on the boat, Phil could have been blown sky high.

There was another time that Phil was affected by a Psychic incident. I recall this particular incident vividly. Phil owned a white Cadillac. For some reason while Phil and I were driving around town, I felt something strange. "Phil," I muttered, "I think you'll have to get rid of this car. There's going to be an accident, a real bad accident. I can't shake this feeling I have."

Phil stared at me in disbelief. "Dayle, this is a brand new car. What do you mean there's going to be an accident?"

"Phil, I can't be any more specific than that. I simply see an accident involving a white Cadillac," I said.

Within two months Phil managed to sell the white Cadillac back to the dealership. He didn't want any bad karma. He hoped that by returning the car to the dealership he could avoid any accidents that might come with the car.

Two months later, Phil's best friend Jerry Campbell and his wife were jogging down a highway in California. They were both hit by a diesel truck and killed instantly. The strange thing about this story is that Phil and Jerry both had purchased white Cadillacs at the same time.

Explanation: This is a common error for many Psychics when we see events that are going to happen. In this particular case, Phil and Jerry both had the same type of car, right down to the same color, make and model.

Jerry and Phil were one; they were best friends. When Jerry died, a part of Phil died also.

I was trying to save the life of my friend, but unbeknownst to me, it would be Phil's best friend's life that would have a fatal ending. I had met Jerry Campbell through Phil on many occasions. I remember he was always afraid of dying young. He never wanted to know his future. Then, on the other hand, there is Phil Simpson . . . always checking out his life with a Psychic so he can make choices of his own free will.

This reminds me of a story. One Psychic said to another Psychic, "You cannot avoid your destiny."

The other replied, "You make your own destiny."

The first Psychic gave an example of a woman who was told that she would die from something hitting her on the head. To escape her fate, she moved to Arizona and made sure there was no possibility of anything falling on her. One day, two children were playing baseball outside her house. The baseball went flying, crashed through a window of her home, and hit her on the head. She died instantly.

The second Psychic gave an example of a woman who consulted with the Psychic before traveling to Las Vegas. The Psychic forewarned the woman not to travel by plane, for there would be a crash. The woman heeded the Psychic's warning and decided to drive to Las Vegas rather than fly. En route she heard of a plane crash involving the same plane she would have been flying on. All passengers were killed instantly.

The first story deals with predestination, the second with free-will choice. No matter what the woman in the first story did, she was fated to die. She could not avoid her destiny.

The second woman chose to live, and death ignored her. There are many different roads we can choose to travel. That's where free will plays a huge role in our lives. Remember, our own choices play a tremendously important part in how we arrive at our destiny.

In the case of Jerry Campbell, he believed in his heart that he had only a short time to live. Somehow this self-fulfilling prophecy came upon him.

On the other hand, Phil Simpson always heeds the warning; therefore, his destiny is one of longevity.

I have learned over the years that a Psychic shouldn't play God and predict death. Many times I receive calls from clients who tell me that another Psychic told them they would die at an early age. I always ask those clients if, at the time of their readings, someone such as a relative or close friend had passed on. The answer is always yes.

You see, many Psychics will tend to pick up on a death that is close to the person they're reading and mistakenly believe it is the client who is going to die.

The only truth here is that death is near. For when someone close passes on, a part of you dies also. It would be wiser for the experienced Psychic to say, "I see a passing in your family; I'm not sure who it may be," rather than scare a person unnecessarily.

Helen's Story

"You're live on the radio with Psychic Dayle Schear," the radio deejay announced. "And our next caller is Helen Haas from South Lake Tahoe."

"Hi, Helen. This is Dayle. How can I help you?"

"Hi, Dayle, I really enjoy your show. I'd like to know about my daughter and how she's doing."

"Helen, what's your daughter's name and where is she located?"

"Her name is Jamie. She's in the Bay Area."

I paused to gather my thoughts. I felt something was wrong. I was uneasy about Helen's question. I stared off into the distance; a rush of fear, an uneasiness, came over me. The feeling was so overwhelming that I forgot that I was live on the radio. The words poured out of my mouth as if I had no control.

"Helen, your daughter's in danger. You must go to her now! She's in an extremely dangerous situation. You must stop what you're doing, jump in your car, and drive to the Bay Area now!" I caught Helen off guard.

She replied as if she were in shock, "Dayle, I have a few days off in a couple of days. Is it all right if I go then? I don't want to lose my job."

"Tomorrow may be too late!" I shouted. You have to get there today, do you understand? Please listen to me; it's a matter of life and death! I see your daughter is on drugs. Correct?"

"Yes," she replied.

"Your daughter has overdosed. I see her lying in a bed, unconscious. Now, do you understand?" I felt like screaming at her.

"Yes. I'll leave now." Helen hung up the phone.

"Whoa!" the deejay remarked. "I sure hope Helen gets there in time. Why don't we go to a commercial break while you pause to gather your thoughts."

During the break he asked, "How do you *know* these things?"

I replied, "I just know. It's a *knowing feeling;* it's stronger than anything or anyone can describe. Sometimes the knowing feeling takes the form of visions; you know, like moving pictures. It's something in your gut that's indicating danger. That's the best way I can describe the feeling."

The deejay and I got engrossed in the topic of *knowing*, and the conversation went on after the show ended shortly after Helen's call.

One week later: I was live on the air once again. The telephone lights were all lit up. The deejay picked up a caller who turned out, much to our surprise, to be Helen.

"Dayle, this is Helen. I called to thank you," she said.

"Thank me for what?" Sometimes when I blurt out things, my memory later fails me. This was one of those times.

"I want to thank you for saving my daughter's life," she said.

The deejay interrupted. "Helen, why don't you tell the listening audience what happened, and bring us up to date."

"Okay," she responded. "Well, you remember last week I called in and spoke to Dayle about my daughter in the Bay Area."

I said, "Oh, now I remember. What happened? Please go on, Helen."

"You see, I'm a maid at the Cedar Lodge in South Lake Tahoe, California. I always listen to Dayle's radio show every Friday afternoon while I'm making my rounds. I decided to call. Most of the time the phone lines are jammed. I've tried on several occasions, and I've never been able to get through. This particular Friday was different. The phone rang and immediately I was the next caller, much to my surprise. I asked Dayle about my daughter Jamie in the Bay Area. She frightened me with her tone of voice. It was as if she was giving me a message and I had no choice but to listen. There was something in her voice that made me respond.

"I quickly found my supervisor and told her there was someone ill in my family; I needed to be let out of work right away. She consented.

"I jumped into my car and went to the Bay Area. It took me about four-and-one-half hours to get there. I stopped at my granddaughter's house and asked her to show me where Jamie lived. We arrived at Jamie's house within fifteen minutes. I knocked on the door and her husband answered. He was bewildered that I was there.

"'What are you doing here?' he asked.

"'I came to see my daughter Jamie. Where is she?' I demanded to see her.

"'She's in the bedroom upstairs,' he responded.

"My granddaughter and I climbed the stairs till we reached Jamie's room. There she was, lying on the bed; she could barely move. There were bruises all over her body. Jamie seemed semi-conscious. I was determined to take her back with me to Lake Tahoe. My granddaughter and I carried her to the car.

"Jamie's husband said, 'By the way, your daughter is crazy. Where are you taking her, anyway?'

"My response was, 'Don't worry; I agree with you. I'm taking her to a mental institution.' That seemed to appease him. We carried Jamie to the car and I placed her in the back seat with my granddaughter and drove off to Tahoe.

"I remember driving for about an hour. It must have been near midnight when, suddenly, my granddaughter started to scream.

"'Grandma, Grandma! Jamie has stopped breathing!'

"I turned and saw my daughter Jamie lying as if in death. I kicked the car into high gear, speeding, looking for the nearest hospital. We were lucky—a hospital was only a mile away. We rushed Jamie into the emergency room.

"The doctor worked on her till she began to breathe on her own. We found out she had overdosed on drugs, just like Dayle said. The doctor told me we got her there just in the nick of time. Her heart had stopped beating and she was dead for about a minute before they revived her.

"Jamie spent one week in the hospital. I stayed by her side every moment till she recovered. We brought her back with us to Lake Tahoe so she could start her life over again.

"If it wasn't for Dayle warning me about my daughter, God only knows what would have happened to her. I wanted to thank you again, Dayle. You gave me back my daughter."

I was speechless, overwhelmed, lost for words. I finally said, "Helen, all that matters is that your daughter is alive."

"Thanks to you, Dayle," she replied.

"No, Helen, thank God, for he gave me this gift to help others."

Helen, Jamie, and her daughters are doing fine. In fact, we have become the best of friends.

Explanation: When Helen called the radio station, I believe she was worried about her daughter Jamie. I picked up on that fear and gazed into the probabilities of Jamie's future. I used remote viewing. Physically, I was in one place, but my mind traveled to where Jamie was living. I was able visually to see Jamie in trouble and in need of someone to help her.

It's not quite as simple as it sounds. I believe that when someone is in trouble, telepathic signals are sent out within the universe. Those thoughts may travel to the closest person who can help the person in need. I was in proximity to Helen, and I was the closest person that she would listen to at that time.

Synchronicity, my friends:
1. Helen turned on the radio and happened to be listening to my show.
2. Even though all the lines were busy, Helen was meant to get through to me.
3. I gave Helen the message that her daughter was in danger.
4. If for some reason Helen didn't act upon my message, her daughter might not be alive today. Helen chose to respond.
5. She drove to the Bay Area for over four hours, not knowing where her daughter lived.

6. Through the help of her granddaughter, she was able to find Jamie's house.
7. Through perfect timing, she was able to drive her daughter to a nearby hospital. Jamie's life was saved.

Synchronicity is the law of the universe. What is meant to be, will be. Remember, if there is a soul to be saved, the messages will be sent out within the universe to find the right person to help the person in need.

Life-saving Remedies

Mrs. Wellington

The phone rang. Blythe answered, and the expression on his face seemed to signal an urgency to this call. Mrs. Wellington was on the other end, calling from New York. "I'd like to set up an appointment with Dayle Schear. Dayle was highly recommended to me. I'll be flying into Honolulu next month. I can't wait to see her," she said. Blythe booked the appointment.

On the appointed day, Mrs. Wellington took the long bus ride from Waikiki to Hawaii Kai. Blythe promptly picked her up at the bus stop and brought her to our house.

Mrs. Wellington was in for a surprise. She had waited well over a month to see me, but I don't think she was prepared for what I was about to tell her.

As the reading began, I asked her to show me some pictures of friends and family that she might be concerned about. Within moments, a terrible feeling came over me. I blurted out, "Excuse me, Mrs. Wellington. Have you been having trouble with your blood pressure?"

"Yes," she replied. "How did you know? But I take medication for it, so I'm not concerned."

"I think you'd better be concerned," I said.

"Don't worry, Dayle, I'll check with my doctor when I get back to New York next week."

"No! You don't understand. You're taking the wrong medication, and I want you to see a doctor today."

Mrs. Wellington seemed shocked at my outburst. "Dayle, please don't worry. I'm fine. Let's continue the reading."

"If you don't get to a doctor today, you could suffer a stroke!" I yelled at her. Mrs. Wellington finally got the message.

"Okay" she agreed. "Do you know of a doctor around here?"

I phoned my doctor and asked if he could see Mrs. Wellington right away.

"No problem," the nurse replied. I asked Blythe to take her to the doctor right away.

Several hours later, I received a phone call from Mrs. Wellington. She couldn't thank me enough. She told me that when the doctor had checked her blood pressure, he found it was in the danger zone. He immediately changed her medication, and she stayed in the office while he monitored her blood pressure. Within an hour her blood pressure went back to normal. The doctor asked, "How did a Psychic know your blood pressure was in the danger area?"

"I don't know," she replied. "I guess she has a gift."

"I guess your Psychic helped save your life. If your blood pressure had gone any higher, we would have had to hospitalize you. You might have had a stroke," he said. "Well, everything is okay now. Let your doctor in New York be aware of the change in medication."

Mrs. Wellington said to me, "Thanks, Dayle. I guess I got a little bit *more* than a reading. I believe in fate; I was meant to see you."

Mrs. Wellington is one of many persons whose lives have been saved by Psychic readings.

Doctor Su

I remember not too long ago a doctor by the name of Dr. Su came to see me. He was a dentist from one of the Outer Islands. When he sat down for his reading, I noticed he was pale. There was some unusual feeling about him, and I searched my mind to find the answer.

"Doctor Su, are you aware that you might have a heart problem?" I asked.

"Yes," he replied. "That's why I came to you. An operation has been suggested, but I don't know what to do. I'm getting up there in age; I'm in my late seventies, Dayle. I don't think I'll live through an operation. What do you see?"

This is a tough decision for a Psychic. I thought, what if I suggest an operation and he dies? If I leave it up to free will, Dr. Su may not get the operation.

I had to ask God to muster up all the power within me for this answer. I said, "Dr. Su, I think you must have this operation, or you may not live another two years. I would suggest you get the best cardiologist, speak with him, tell him your fears, and see what he says. If you undergo surgery at this time, you'll be fine and extend your life."

I spoke with authority. There seemed to be a knowing sense about what I was telling the doctor. I also knew in my heart that when he left the reading, he would do whatever he wanted to do, anyway. My job was to guide him.

Several months had passed when Dr. Su called to thank me for everything I had recommended. He had gone through with the operation and all had gone well. He couldn't thank me enough. Dr. Su is still alive today, five years later.

When I first started reading clients, I didn't realize the concerns they have regarding health matters. In the beginning of my career, there were times I was not strong enough to demand that a client see a doctor. I felt this was up to the client.

Because I did not push them, I lost two of my clients. One was a friend who I had warned repeatedly of high blood pressure. He chose to ignore me. He remarked that if that was the way he was supposed to die, so be it. I just wish he had listened.

When the other client came to see me, I asked if he was having blood pressure problems as well. The client lied and said, "I'm in the best of health after you warned me last time." I believed him, although later that day I made a comment to my husband, "It sure is funny, but I can't see his future." Thinking my ability was off, I asked the client to come back another day. I can't monitor everyone. That evening he died due to a massive stroke.

In the years that followed, I made a firm commitment not to take matters so lightly if I saw health problems in anyone that I read for. Today when I do readings, especially business readings, I always tell my clients that I have to check them out on a personal level first. That way I can monitor their health. If there is a problem, health-wise, I will make sure they do something about it, or my reading will not continue. You see, I'm dedicated to my field. I'm in the business of *saving lives.*

CHAPTER 8

IT SHOULD ONLY HAPPEN TO YOU

I was twenty-five years old, married, and wondering where my life was going. I decided to try my luck at acting in the big city of Los Angeles.

During my short-lived acting career, I worked as an extra in several grade-B movies. On a movie called *Lifeguard,* the extras gathered on set, waiting patiently for our segment. The wait was endless, sometimes eight hours to do a five-minute shoot. While we waited, we would begin to chat with others, and within moments we would find ourselves deep in discussion with strangers.

Little did I know that one stranger I was to encounter would play a major role in how my life would turn out. I was approached by a handsome man in his forties. He was tall in stature, had dark brown hair and a mustache, and was very appealing.

"Young lady," he said, "have we met somewhere before? You look very familiar to me."

"No, I don't think so," I replied.

"Well, allow me to introduce myself. My name is Don Torres. And your name?" he asked.

"My name is Dayle Schear."

"Nice to make your acquaintance. I hope you don't think I'm prying, but I have a strange question to ask you. Has your right knee been bothering you?"

"My right knee?" What a bizarre thing to say, I thought. "No, I don't think so. Why would you ask about my right knee? Although, it's funny you should ask; when I was younger I dislocated my right knee on several occasions."

"I thought so," he said. "Well, I see your knee will dislocate again in the future." Don walked away.

"Hey, wait a minute. Come back. Are you Psychic?" I chased after him.

He turned and stared at me. "Look deep into my eyes, young lady. You should know the answer to that question. For, you see, it takes one to know one. You, my child, are gifted. The only problem is, you don't know you have this gift that will someday help thousands of people. You don't belong here."

The next thing I knew, Don was called on set. He disappeared from my life. I approached my long-time friend and acting partner, Sam Veta. "Sam, see that guy over there? Have you ever seen him before? Do you know anything about him?"

"He's a Psychic, Dayle. Didn't you know?"

"No," I replied.

"Why do you ask?"

"Well, I think he read my future, or maybe it was my past," I replied in amazement.

"Did he tell you that you would be famous?"

"No, Sam, he told me my right knee was going to dislocate."

"Charming fellow. Oh, well, don't take these things so seriously." Sam seemed bewildered.

Several weeks later I was called for a movie called *Lepeke,* starring Tony Curtis. I was excited; I couldn't wait to meet him. I immediately picked up the phone and dialed Sam's number. "Sam, were you called for *Lepeke?*"

"Yes," he replied. "I can't wait. This is the most exciting moment of our lives. I bet we're going to make it big, Dayle. I have this funny feeling that something good is going to happen for us in this movie."

Sam was the perpetual dreamer, always planning how he would make it big in the movies. He wanted to make it more than anyone else I have ever met, to the point where his dreams overpowered him. Sam would make sure his face was in every shot of the movie. On the other hand, I found acting amusing. The pay was good and, of course, there was always plenty of food around. Plus, it was a monumental way to meet the Hollywood stars.

Within a few days we were on the set of *Lepeke* with Tony Curtis, my idol. Sam and I had a bet going, on who would meet Tony first. I, of course, won. The director noticed me and asked me if I would like to be in a scene with Tony Curtis.

"Yes!" I replied eagerly.

"Follow me," he said. "You see that ferris wheel up there? I want you to sit next to Tony in the ferris wheel scene." This was my big break. Sam was right. But, wait a minute, that ferris wheel is several hundred feet off the ground, I thought to myself. I'm scared of heights. What am I going to do?

"Everyone on set," the director blared. "You, over there. Hey, you, young lady, it's time to take your place next to Tony Curtis. Go on, climb aboard the ferris wheel. Tony's waiting."

"Wait a minute, sir; can I talk to you?"

"Now what's the matter? Here I'm giving you the chance of a lifetime, and you're blowing it. What's wrong with you?"

"I'm scared of heights. I can't go up on that thing," I replied.

The director shouted and pointed to the ferris wheel. "If you don't go up there, you're fired!"

"Okay," I replied nonchalantly. "I'm not going on that ferris wheel." I was creating a scene.

Tony Curtis rushed to my aid. "What's all the commotion about? What's the matter, darling?"

"I'm scared of heights. I get motion sickness."

The director overheard the conversation and burst into laughter. "Okay, young lady, take your place in the crowd. I'll find someone else."

"Tony, I warn you; it's going to be a rough ride," I remarked.

The scene began. I watched intently as the ferris wheel spun round and round in a circular motion. Then the wheel stopped. Out of the corner of my eye I noticed a barf bag being brought in for the star. Thank God I had decided to hold my ground.

Much to my surprise, the director became fond of me. As the scene progressed, he promoted me to more detailed roles.

The next scene was of the Roaring Twenties. Since my mom and dad were of that era, I had learned to do the Charleston at a very early age, and I was quite good at it. The director noticed and paired me up with an actor on set. The music began. I finally had my own scene. Sam was right again. I danced and danced. My partner and I were really into it. Then Tony Curtis made his way down the staircase and approached me. His role called for him to grab me away from my partner. The scene changed rapidly.

All of a sudden, without any warning, I collapsed. I was lying on the floor, unable to get up. My knee was dislocated. There was a commotion on the set. I can't believe this is happening to me, I thought. Why? After crawling on the ground, I somehow managed to pop my knee back into place. Someone appeared on set with an ace elastic bandage. The director pleaded with me to try to finish the scene. I complied.

That was the end of my acting career. I was laid up for well over eight weeks, hobbling along on crutches. The thought entered my mind that I had to find that Psychic, Don Torres. I placed a call to Sam and asked him, "You know that Psychic we met on set? How can I find him?"

"Dayle, have you ever thought about looking him up in the phone book?"

"Great idea, Sam, why didn't I think of that?" I said.

"By the way, you're the talk of the studio. I knew you were going to get a break, but I didn't think it would be so soon." Sam chuckled.

"Thanks, Sam, I guess it's up to you now. Besides, you're going to win the bet and become famous well before I will. I have to hang up now. Keep me informed."

I have to find that Psychic, I thought to myself. I searched the phone book, looking for one Don Torres, Psychic. There he was, right smack in the middle of the phone book. I dialed the number with anticipation. The phone rang. "Don Torres' office. May I help you?"

Fortunately, I was able to get an appointment. This would be my first real reading with a Psychic. I knew that Don was for real, and I couldn't wait, although I was scared to death.

I arrived at the office, paid the receptionist fifty dollars, and hobbled with my crutches into the reading room. There sat Don

Torres behind a desk. He asked me to relax and sit comfortably in the chair.

"I remember you," he said. "You're the girl I met on the set of *Lepeke*."

"Yes, Don, and do you remember telling me that my knee would dislocate? Well, here I am, crutches and all."

Don laughed.

The reading began: "Dayle, I see you will become famous. I see you'll be traveling. It looks like you'll be living in one state and traveling to another state. I see you dealing with more money than you have ever dealt with in a lifetime. There will be a divorce."

"Wait, Don," I interrupted. "Does this divorce have to happen? I mean, I've been married to my husband for eight years."

"Dayle, this divorce will be a free-will choice," he replied. Then he asked, "Who is Gerry?"

"Gerry is an entertainer I've been involved with on and off for several years," I answered.

"Gerry . . . Gerry . . . you mean, THE Gerry Turner?"

"Yes."

"Well, Dayle, in the future, I see the two of you having an affair. However, I don't see you marrying this man. Gerry does care about you. The timing is off. You know what I mean."

Don continued. "There will be two deaths in the family. One you know about; the other you don't. The fame I see for you is lined with gold. You will have your own television talk show. There will be three books that you will write. Your Psychic ability will develop, and you'll become famous and prominent. Are there any more questions?"

"Yes, my dad is in the hospital. Will he recover?"

"Yes, he will."

The reading was over. My head began to swim. Fame? Is this man off the deep end? I was in my late twenties, married, and a housewife. Where was all this fame coming from? What kind of Psychic was he? I was infuriated. I had no intentions of ever getting divorced. As I drove home, my anger grew deeper. This man is nuts, I told myself; I'm going to stop payment on his check. And I did.

Little did I know how right-on Don was. The reading I received from him projected fifteen years or so into the future. In fact, some of the things he told me are still happening right now. The proof is in the book that I am writing, as the words make their way to this paper.

Don told me that I would live in one state and work in another. Every day for five years I traveled the highway from my home in South Lake Tahoe, California, to Stateline, Nevada, to work for Harvey's casino as a blackjack dealer. I dealt with more money than most people ever would see in a lifetime.

Don spoke of divorce. In the late 1980s, I divorced my husband Bob.

Don spoke of two deaths in my family; one I would know about, the other I would not. My father passed on shortly after he recovered from prostate cancer. My nephew died, much to our surprise, from a simple operation.

Don spoke of television and talk shows. Twice a year I have a talk show in Honolulu, Hawaii. Fame was definitely in the picture.

There would be three books I would write, he said. Well, *Dare to Be Different!* was my first book. *The Psychic Within* is my second. And I have an idea for my third.

Almost everything Don spoke of has come to pass, with an amazing accuracy of ninety-five percent. The motto of this story is, give a Psychic a chance. Sometimes things don't always happen right away. The anger I had harbored all those years was simply because I could not see the things Don foretold for me. After all, I was just a housewife, happily married.

Within ten years, most of Don's predictions came true. Some of his predictions are still coming true. Throughout the years I have tried endlessly to locate Don Torres. My guilt about stopping payment on his check has been eating away at me. I hope in the future to find him and give him triple his money back.

I learned an important lesson in life. Sometimes you have to trust somebody. Besides my teacher Peter Hurkos, Don Torres was the most accurate Psychic I ever encountered.

Might I say, strange events do happen to me. It was in the fall of 1991. My husband Blythe and I were in Honolulu, eating at one of our favorite restaurants, when lo and behold, in walks Tony Curtis himself. Much to my surprise, I found myself staring at him. He had aged but was still quite handsome.

"Blythe," I said, poking my husband. "Look! It's Tony Curtis!" I was excited to see him.

Tony stared at me as if he knew me but couldn't quite place me. He stopped at my table, reached for my hand, and kissed it gently—a real ladies' man. He smiled and looked right into my eyes.

"My, my, I see a pink Cadillac in your future," he said. Tony was acknowledging that he had seen my television shows in Hawaii. I smiled back. Instead of saying a simple thank you, I had to blurt out, "Tony, remember *Lepeke*?"

A puzzled look crossed his face. "Yes," he replied.

"Well, do you remember the ferris wheel scene? I was the girl who warned you not to go on the ferris wheel."

Tony paused and rubbed his forehead. "I'm sorry, I really don't remember." He started to walk away from my table. Then he turned abruptly and came dashing back to the table. He pointed his finger at me and said excitedly, "I do remember! Oh, yes, I do!" He walked away, shaking his head and smiling.

I never imagined in my wildest dreams that I would ever come face to face with Tony Curtis again and have the chance to bring up memories of the ferris wheel scene. But stranger things have happened!

As for my acting partner, Sam Veta, he became Dudley Moore's personal confidant and secretary, and we still keep in touch. Sam is still determined to make it in the movies. He doesn't understand that he has already made it.

CHAPTER 9

EXPERIENCING THE UNUSUAL

The life of a Psychic is filled with intrigue, danger and the unusual. Sometimes I find myself peacefully reading a book, all cozy and warm, sitting by the fireplace, and within moments the telephone rings and I'm off to New York working on a murder case. I must admit that throughout the years I have found my work rewarding and spontaneous. I would like to relate several stories from through the years, which I found to be very interesting.

Norreen from Alaska

It was somewhere in the 1980s when I first met Norreen. I remember her well. I had a radio talk show in Hawaii when Norreen visited the Islands. She just happened to turn on the radio, and there I was. Shortly after the radio show, Norreen booked an appointment with me.

She arrived at my apartment in Waikiki the next day. I showed her to the reading room and asked her to relax. Norreen mentioned she was from Alaska. "How nice," I responded. She asked the usual questions regarding her family. She wanted to know how things would be going in her husband's business. The key word here was *husband*. While she was talking about her husband's business, my thoughts began to wander.

"Dayle, can you tell me if my husband's business will be all right this year?" she asked.

"Norreen, your husband's business is fine. That's not the problem."

"What's the problem?" she asked.

"I don't know if I should tell you," I replied.

"Are you picking up something bad?" She was beginning to worry.

I paused. I had to mull over this situation in my mind. I finally blurted out, "Norreen, are you aware that your husband is having an affair?"

"No! Are you sure? I've suspected something going on, but I just couldn't put my finger on it. I'm astonished," she said. "Can you describe the girl?"

"Yes, I can. The girl works in his office. She has long black hair and is young. Does this make sense to you?" I asked.

"Yes, sort of. The person you're describing is his secretary. Is it her?"

"That's hard for me to tell without a picture," I said. Norreen stood up to leave. "Dayle, I have to go now. I think I want to call my husband in Alaska. I'll get back to you."

Two weeks later Norreen telephoned me. "Dayle, this is Norreen, the lady from Alaska. Remember me?"

"Yes, how are things in Alaska?" I asked.

"Dayle, I'm not in Alaska; I'm in Hawaii," she said. "I need to see you. It's urgent!"

"Hawaii!" I was surprised. "Didn't you go back to Alaska?"

"I'll tell you all about it when I see you. Do you have any openings? I'm staying across the street at the Ilikai Hotel."

"Norreen, it's funny that you called. I just had a cancellation. Why don't you come up now!"

"I'm on my way," she said.

While Norreen was on her way to my apartment, I flashed back into the reading I had given Norreen about her husband's affair. This is unusual for me. Normally, when a person leaves my apartment, the reading leaves right along with the individual. I tend to wipe it out of my mind so I can focus on the next person. This was different. I remembered. I had felt bad telling Norreen about her husband; I didn't want to be a home wrecker. Yet, if I had lied to her, I would have been an unethical Psychic. I knew she would find out about her husband eventually. It would have been sad if she found out five years later; then, she would have wasted a lot of years. My motto is to be honest. When people come to me for a reading, they had better be prepared. I tell them what I see and counsel them along the way.

The doorbell rang. I let Norreen in. "Dayle, you're not going to believe this," she said.

"Try me."

"Well, after the last reading, I left your apartment and walked across the street to the Ilikai Hotel. I was in shock. I placed a call to my husband in Alaska, and I asked him how things were going.

"'Fine,' he said. I told him I had been to a Psychic in Hawaii. He had the nerve to ask what you saw for him. I told him you saw him having an affair with his secretary!"

"Now, wait a minute, Norreen. I didn't exactly say that," I remarked.

"I know, Dayle, but this was the only way I could get something out of him. I had to use you."

"Go on," I said.

"There was a long pause on the phone, then he answered me.

"'Norreen, your Psychic is right; I am having an affair,' he said.

"'Are you kidding or are you just appeasing me?' I asked.

"'No, I'm telling you the truth.'

"I was bewildered. I didn't know what to say. He told me the affair with his secretary had been going on for a while now. He wanted to tell me but couldn't—he was glad that I had learned it from a Psychic; it relieved him of the pressure. I asked if he wanted a divorce; he didn't know. Then he had the audacity to ask me to ask you if he would end up with his secretary! The egotistical son of a bitch! That's why I'm here. I never left Hawaii. I've been sitting in my room all this time thinking.

"Dayle, what's going to happen?"

I said, "Sit down, Norreen. Let me do a reading on you."

The reading began: "Norreen, I see your husband is going to continue the affair with his secretary. Eventually, he's going to ask for a divorce. I don't think you can avoid any of this. I really don't know what to tell you. I feel bad about your marriage and how this whole situation came about.

"You must prepare yourself mentally. I see you meeting another man in the future, someone you will marry. Eventually, you'll be very happy with this other man. But there is much turmoil you'll have to go through first."

After the reading, Norreen left my apartment. It wasn't until 1984, three years later, that we met again.

This time I was doing a show at Harrah's in Reno, Nevada. There was a knock on my dressing room door just before show time. A lady appeared. I seemed to recognize her from a distance.

She introduced herself to me, "Hi, Dayle, I'm Norreen from Alaska. Do you remember me?"

Norreen from Alaska. I searched my mind. "Yes, I do! How did you find me?"

"I was in Reno," she said, "and I happened to look up at the billboard of Harrah's while I was walking. I stopped dead in the street and stared at the name on the billboard. I knew it was you. I had to see you. Can you please give me a reading before you go on stage, please?"

"After the show, I'll be glad to," I said.

Two hours later, after the show, I met with Norreen. She brought me up to date regarding her marriage. I gave her a reading well into the future. Included were the initials of a man she would be involved with. I explained to her that her husband was pretty close to becoming bankrupt.

"That he is," she replied. Norreen explained that the girl her husband was having an affair with had left him. He wanted Norreen back, but it was too late; she no longer trusted him. She thanked me for the help and knowledge I had given her. She was on her way back to Alaska to pack up the rest of her things.

After that reading our paths never crossed again. I think of Norreen often and wonder how she is doing. It's funny how Psychics can play a role in people's lives. I guess this was just meant to be.

Crissy Kengla's
Just-a-Thank-You Letter to Psychic Dayle Schear

Having knowledge of Psychics most of my life, I feel most of their predictions were possibly fifty percent accurate. I've gauged the self-professed Psychics whom I have met as averaging seven on a scale of ten. As a young girl, I always was attracted to anyone with the least bit of extrasensory powers. By the time I was seventeen years of age, I had encountered more than your normal share of Psychics.

I would venture to say that Psychic Dayle Schear could measure 9.8 on the "ESP Power Scale." I have based my conclusions on facts and various Psychic readings that were given to my husband, H.P. Kengla, as well as to myself.

We met Psychic Dayle Schear while attending real estate school in South Lake Tahoe. Dayle seemed to be drawn to us for some reason. I remember her first remarks to me. "Crissy, I know you're Psychic. You have an ability that is uncanny." We became the best of friends and invited Dayle to our house in the Tahoe Keys.

When Dayle started to seat herself at our dining table, she made the astounding comment that the overhead green Tiffany lamp came from a brothel. We knew the oil-lamp-converted-into-electrical had come from a brothel in South San Francisco. The lamp belonged to the parents of Grafton Worthington from 1905 through 1945.

Many predictions were made for our family by Psychic Dayle Schear. I came to the deduction that God had been using this young lady as a medium since she was a teenager.

Watching Dayle's Psychic ability cultivate each year was like watching a healthy child grow mentally and emotionally in stature. A small town like Lake Tahoe does encourage creativity. Dayle had to learn to share her gift of vision in her own way.

My husband H.P. was a pilot. He founded one of the first two airlines in the Lake Tahoe area, Paradise Airlines and Holiday Airlines. Dayle merged into the picture when H.P. and I were on the verge of bankruptcy. H.P. thought he would never fly again. Moping around the house, H.P. asked Dayle to come down to Tahoe Keys and give him a reading.

Through Dayle's readings on H.P. Kengla, she foretold that he would be flying once again. She saw him flying in Florida. H.P. hated the state of Florida. He thought Dayle was off her rocker. Two years later H.P. rang me long distance from Florida merely to ask me to call Dayle and apologize for protesting her prediction so avidly.

Three-and-one-half years later, H.P.'s employer sold out to another airline. H.P. once again was out of a job. Dayle stated, "In two months and two days you will be flying in Indonesia." Now H.P. really flipped out. Dayle's far-fetched visions were usually exact, but this one had to be a mistake or misread. H.P was in shock. However, in exactly two months and two days, H.P landed in Jakarta, Indonesia, to train pilots on three aircraft that once belonged to him. Once again an apology was in order.

Usually in January or August, Dayle would give H.P. readings by gently holding the bottom of his right foot. Dayle continually warned H.P. that he should have his stomach checked out; she saw danger in the stomach area. Dayle forewarned him on *many* occasions that she saw a growth in the stomach area.

"H.P., I want you to pay attention to me. This could be a matter of life or death," she said. However, all H.P. wanted to do was fly.

This prediction of Psychic Dayle Schear came to pass as well. This was one prediction I didn't want to hear. Seven years later, after many warnings and all too much suffering about his health, H.P. passed on of stomach cancer.

Dayle continued to read for me. The most astounding prediction for me was envisioned by Dayle in 1981 before the passing of H.P. Dayle stated I would become a hermit in the future. All my friends rolled on the floor with laughter. Crissy become a hermit?

Well, the idea that the world's number-one party-loving socialite airline stewardess, who spent every waking moment in the middle of the world full of people, was to become a *hermit?* Why, the very idea!

I soon learned after H.P.'s passing that life was not fun anymore. I decided to attend San Diego College for a year to take my mind off of things. I returned to the home H.P and I built. I realized that all the people with whom I socialized were vultures. Half my life had been lived expressly for H.P.

Fate had now dealt a new hand, and I decided she who travels alone travels fastest and best. I, in fact, became a hermit. Dayle's visions have more than endured. This Psychic, Dayle Schear, truly has a gift, and she will go on helping many people.

Thank you Dayle for helping guide the Kengla family.

Crissy and I became the best of friends for years to follow. This lady truly has a heart and was helping thousands of people in her own way. She gave when there was nothing left to give. When the money ran out, so did Crissy's friends. She learned a long, hard lesson. The trusting Crissy finally became aware that it was time to nurse herself back to health. I will always love and cherish Crissy from the bottom of my heart, and I know that H.P. guides us from above.

A Test of Faith

It was the early part of the 1980s. I remember the day and year well. I would embark on a turning point in my life, a point that would change part of my life, including my soul.

I was married to my first husband, Bob, a blackjack dealer for Harrah's in Lake Tahoe. I worked for the Sahara Hotel as a telephone operator. The telephone operators were located in the basement of the hotel for security purposes. Just in case there might be a bomb in the hotel, we were safely tucked away so no harm could come to us. One needed all types of security keys and ingenious devices in order to enter our room. The security guards made sure there were no unauthorized people in the hallway.

As I drove to work on that particular day, I was in a severe state of depression. I remember my dog had suffered a stroke and was lying in the pet hospital. I have this incredible love for animals, and I can't bear to see them hurt in any way. I had prayed for weeks to God, asking for her to be saved, but my dog didn't seem to be getting any better. We also had been plagued with several deaths within the family at that time. I recall I was beginning to lose my faith in God. I was questioning in my mind whether God ever existed.

When I arrived at work, I took up my normal post answering the phones. Within an hour of my arrival, a security guard opened our door. I glanced up at this man when he spoke. "Hi, my name is Darryl. I'm just checking on you girls to make sure everything is okay."

I looked straight into Darryl's eyes. He stared at me for a moment and said, "You're Psychic, aren't you?"

Startled, I answered, "Yes."

Darryl's eyes were astounding. They turned from brown into a bright *red*. He frightened me.

I turned away from him abruptly and faced my operating board as he left. I thought to myself, how did he know I was Psychic? I never told anyone.

I was terrified of this person.

My shift ended. Instead of going home, for some reason I was compelled to head toward the cafeteria. There was Darryl sitting there, waiting for me. He asked me to have a seat. "I've been waiting for you," he said. "I need to speak with you. Please sit down for a moment."

I felt as though I were hypnotized. I sat down next to him, listening as he spoke.

"I know you're Psychic," he said decisively.

"How do you know?" I said.

"Don't interrupt me. This is hard enough for me to tell you. Let me speak."

I remained quiet and listened intently.

"You're being tested; that's why I'm here. You see, I've come from the other side, the dark side. You represent the good; I represent evil. I want to go back to the good side. I want you to help me cross over. I want you to help me. You know what I mean."

I started to get up from the table, frightened by what this lunatic was saying. "I'm sorry, Darryl, I can't help you. There's no way back for you. I'm not the one. I don't have the answers. *I can't help you!"*

I tried to stand up and leave the table, but I was stopped! There was a force field around me, and I couldn't move—I was paralyzed. I had never experienced anything like this before. I wanted to run, but the energy stopped me. I was compelled to stare into Darryl's eyes until this energy released me. Perspiration rolled down my forehead. I was helpless. Within moments the force field stopped. Every ounce of my being was emptied, drained of energy. I was exhausted.

Darryl stared at me. "Dayle, did you feel that energy?"

"Yes, what was that?" I asked, somewhat shaken.

Darryl smirked and said, "You've won this time. Your energy is pure; it comes from God himself. *I told you I was sent here to test you.* I was sent here with hopes you would follow me. My mission was to bring you back to the other side. Someday I'll be back. You know I can give you anything you want in life if only you'll follow me."

My response was quick and firm. "Darryl, there isn't anything I want badly enough in this world that you or your people can give me. No, Darryl, I'll never cross over to the side of darkness, the side of evil. I learned something very important tonight. You're right, I lost my faith in God for a brief moment in time, but you restored my faith. For if there is evil such as what I experienced within you, then there must be a God." The strange conversation ended. I was free to go.

I raced home to Bob. I couldn't wait to tell him what had happened. Bob listened intently as I spoke. I repeated word for word what happened that day. The look on Bob's face was one of astonishment.

Bob couldn't explain what I had been through that afternoon. But he knew my faith in God was totally restored. Miraculously, within days my dog was healed. Bob asked me to check up on Darryl, to find out more about him.

The next day I went to work just a little bit early. I checked with the personnel department to see when Darryl had been hired. I didn't want to run into him again. The personnel department told me that no such person ever worked for Sahara Hotel as a security guard. Darryl never existed.

This one incident in my life was not a dream; it was real. I searched for answers. I wanted to find out why this was happening to me. Was there such a thing as the devil? Did he really exist? Was he disguised in another person's body? All these questions and more haunted me for many years to come.

It wasn't until many years had passed that I had my answers. Peter Hurkos had sent me to his teacher, Dr. Andrija Puharich, in North Carolina, for testing.

The time I spent with Andrija gave me all my answers. I remember firing the questions at him. I asked about this man that I had met. I wanted to know if he was real. Andrija explained he was very real; in fact, I had manifested him. He told me that because I had lost my faith in God at that time, I needed answers to prove to myself that there was more to life. Therefore, I created the situation with Darryl and made him exist. Darryl was there solely for the purpose of proving to me that I shouldn't give up hope or faith in God. Andrija explained that there is good and evil in everything. You can drink a glass of water in thirst, or you can drown in water. You can take a knife and eat with it, or you can take a knife and kill someone. There is a dark side of the world, and I just happened to tap into that. As long as I stayed on the right path, God and spirit would guide me.

The words of Andrija stayed with me. Darryl or the likes of him never appeared again.

CHAPTER 10

A CHILD IS MISSING

Sometimes a Personal Letter Can Say It All

This is just one of many letters that I receive on a daily basis:

May 10,1992: Dear Dayle Schear, It's been one week since you helped us find our precious fourteen-year-old, runaway daughter, Pollyann. I hope that this letter does some justice in letting you know how grateful and thankful we are to you, for bringing home our special "Baby girl."

A long time ago when we first heard of Psychics, we never really paid much attention to them. Unbeknownst to us, we were to gain deep respect and belief in such a talent such as yours.

On April 25th, 1992, Pollyann was dropped off by her father Thomas at Pearlridge Shopping Center. There she was to meet her friends to celebrate her birthday. Afterwards, they were to head towards the Ice Palace for some ice skating. Pollyann was instructed to call home before going to the Ice Palace, so that one of us could give her and some of her friends a ride. However, that night Pollyann never called home. We worriedly searched Pearlridge and the Ice Palace but couldn't find her. We felt something was wrong, so we started to call some of her friends, but they too had not seen nor talked to Pollyann that day. By two in the morning of April 26,1992 we reported Pollyann missing to the Honolulu Police Department.

For whatever reason, HPD listed Pollyann as a runaway. Two days had passed and Pollyann had not returned. Her case was turned over to the Juvenile Crime Prevention Division. We were then informed by the detective to refer all our leads and any new information to them or call 911. Pollyann's case was to be entered into the HPD computer, and should some kind of attention be brought out in the open in regards to her, the officer would then check the computer.

The police seemed to think Pollyann would involve herself in some offensive situation so that she could be picked up. HPD never publicized the case in any way, shape or form. Nor was the media brought in. Pollyann was just another runaway.

Word arrived several days later from Pollyann's friend Nina. She told us that Pollyann had planned to take a trip with some Brotherhood members to L.A. Naturally, we feared for our daughter's life and well-being. We called the officer in charge. He wanted us to check the airlines to see if Pollyann had boarded a plane. Of course we got nowhere fast, since the airlines don't give out that information. It seemed to me the detective couldn't care less about our daughter. We asked the officer again for suggestions and help! He complained about the time and energy it would take to check the airlines himself. He stated that as soon as we had proof that Pollyann did indeed board a plane, then he would be able to alert authorities in L.A. In the meantime, my husband Thomas worked by day and we searched together by night.

A week after Pollyann's disappearance, a friend of yours, Dayle, informed me that you were willing to help us find our daughter. We were desperate and just wanted to find our little girl. We were ready and willing to try anything.

I recall our first meeting with you at your home in Hawaii Kai. You asked us to bring articles of clothing and/or any items Pollyann had used or touched. As you touched Pollyann's clothing item by item, you were sensing something unusual, but you couldn't put your finger on what it was. You mentioned that drugs were involved with Pollyann. You also mentioned how drugs affect the mind, sometimes making it impossible for a Psychic to track a missing person.

On our second meeting with you, Dayle, you saw things more clearly. You held within the palm of your hands Pollyann's retainer. Pollyann used her retainer every day. You spoke openly about how Pollyann's retainer kept vibrating in your hands. You then made the statement that Pollyann was alive. Relief! I somehow regained my hope about my little girl.

Your visions of Pollyann became clear as you saw her roaming from house to house. You saw her in a car with a man, possibly a military man. You saw Pollyann with male gangsters, men in black jackets. You were picking up on Red Hill. You picked up strong vibes of Pollyann in a home near water with many lights.

Dayle, you mentioned Pollyann was afraid and confused, something about prison and abortion. You saw Pollyann drinking booze. Your strongest vibes at the time were centered in Kalihi.

Dayle, you mentioned that you began to feel high for some reason as you touched Pollyann's lipstick. You were getting lightheaded. It was then you asked us to leave. You needed to be left alone in peace and quiet to concentrate. You mentioned you didn't want telepathy to interfere. We understood and left for the evening.

Several hours later we received a phone call from you. You explained how you were holding in your hand Pollyann's retainer as you sat at your computer. With retainer in hand, you started to channel information. In essence you let yourself be used as a medium for the purpose of finding Pollyann. You sat quietly at the computer and asked for help from your departed teacher, Peter Hurkos. This information is the exact translation that was relayed to us that evening.

Dayle's channeled session with Peter Hurkos concerning our daughter Pollyann:

Pollyann, where are you?

Peter, please help locate Pollyann. Please give me information about this girl. Is she dead or alive?

What is this new frequency that I am feeling?

"Pollyann is alive. She is angry. She wants to teach everyone a lesson for hurting her feelings. She also feels she does not belong here. She wants to leave. She does not want to face the school system or the probation officer. She has been screwing around a lot with a boy who wears a military uniform or screwing around on a military base. She is being hidden and well-protected. House by water, there are city lights. She was at Red Hill; she could still be there. She has been in and out of cars. She seems to be getting ready to go home. She is getting tired of all this and wants things to change for her. The girl is very confused. There is a birthmark on the girl, also a knife from her cutting herself at one time or a scar. However, she is safe in a home. She feels she will be put into a foster home and that no one wants her. There is drinking and drugs involved. Her old neighborhood or in Red Hill, there is something connected to Kalihi, either a friend or someone who can hide her, there. I see a dark car that surrounds her, a black car that she has use of or someone picks her up in. I see a man in military involved or a police officer. She is just a runaway and will return.

"The frequency you are picking up is from the other side. It is a clear channel blocking you from finding her, for she does not want to be found. You pick up her fear, and that will block your ESP. If you follow the frequency, it can lead to the girl. A map is no good. Get in a car and search for her.

Peter, talk to me about Pollyann. Is this really you? Please give me a message.

"Red Hill, near city lights, near military base overlooking the city. Many boys involved; she is trying to find a boy. Or she is *with a boy. Loss of transmission in her brain. There are dead spots, hard to track, could be drugs, could be drinking, could be confusion. She is living off of candy bars. Soon she will be found."*

This information was given to me, Elizabeth Pangelinan, two days before Pollyann was found.

Sunday the 2nd, two days later, the most amazing thing happened. Dayle, do you remember you called our home and told me to go to Pearlridge Shopping Center *now!* You stated that Pollyann would be hanging around there between the hours of 2 o'clock and 5 p.m. By your instructions I did go to Pearlridge when the stores were opened on Sunday the 2nd. I cruised all of Pearlridge and was tired by 11 a.m. I went home for lunch and planned to check Red Hill later. I felt I had to call you, Dayle, to keep you informed of what was happening so far. You urged me to go back to Pearlridge until 5 o'clock when the stores started closing. I was really exhausted, but obeyed. Your husband Blythe instructed me to think only positive thoughts of Pollyann, to concentrate on her and use telepathy, mind-to-mind contact, to draw my daughter to me. I diligently obeyed once again.

When I returned to Pearlridge, I sat. I saw some teenagers walking to Carnival Carnival across the street from where I was. I didn't know it then, but my daughter was in that group. At the time I kept wishing that she would be in that group. My daughter told me later that she had gone outdoors to have a smoke. (Chills, chills, chills.) Tired at my post, I went to the third floor above Christina's and waited some more. I saw a girl in a black jacket with a Badboy emblem on her back. She looked like a gang member. The girl looked around, as if scanning the area to clear the coast. I thought of Pollyann. The girl left, and I thought of following her in hopes she would lead me right to Pollyann. But I had to call home to check and see if everything was okay with my son. The girl went towards Sears and I went in the opposite direction to the phone booth. After my call, I turned cautiously and slowly, even concealing myself behind and in front of passersby. My mind nearly *exploded* when I spotted my daughter's left calf. She was facing the other way. I walked right up behind my daughter. I put my right arm around her neck in a hugging way and glanced at my watch . . . Dayle, it was only moments to 5 p.m.!!!

In the back of my mind I kept screaming, "You did it, Dayle! You found my girl! You really did it!" I am overcome with chills as I type this part of this letter.

After questioning Pollyann, we found out she did meet some of her old time friends at Pearlridge. She subsequently met and made other friends (males), just as you stated. Time was passing. There were three girls, two of them fourteen and the other seventeen years old. The boys were ranging in age from fifteen to eighteen years old. The majority of teenagers were minors and runaways, according to Pollyann. They were living life for the moment, as she explained. The guy she was involved with is not military. But get this, he had an aunt living on the Naval Base at Pearl Harbor, near water, where he took Pollyann on several occasions. That week she was missing, he took Pollyann to her friend's brother's house in Kalihi. Oh! Oh! The house in Pearl Harbor is located near the Moanalua Hwy. At night with all the cars passing by, there were a great *deal of lights* .

Pollyann was *afraid,* just like you stated, about going to a detention home for previous incidents she committed in school, plus the fact she ran away, and she was just too confused about it all. She had sex with this guy she was running around with. They had mentioned *abortion* in case she got pregnant.

Dayle, several uniformed and undercover cops had stopped Pollyann and questioned her about her smoking and drinking beer on several occasions while she was missing. But they never checked her in the computer to see if she was missing. Pollyann mentioned she gave her real name and acted smart with them, but they just told her not to get in trouble! Pollyann would be an easy name to remember because it's so uncommon, especially here in Hawaii.

The police at the Pearl City Station know of our disappointment in them. I mentioned you to Pollyann's probation officer. She was *surprised,* how you helped me find Pollyann. The news of how you helped us will spread like wildfire.

Dayle, words alone cannot express how we feel. We are grateful to you and we love you.

Mahalo Again.
Gratefully yours,
Thomas & Elizabeth Pangelinan

Within a week of Pollyann's return, Elizabeth called and asked if she could bring Pollyann to my home. I said yes. I wanted to question Pollyann about my reading. Daughter, mother and father arrived at my door. I asked to talk to Pollyann in private.

"Pollyann, how do you feel about a Psychic being able to locate you?" I asked.

Pollyann was very evasive, not trusting me at all. "Dayle, I was blown away. Does that answer your question?"

"Yes, but I have a few questions of my own, Pollyann," I replied. "When I was holding your retainer, I was squeezing the hell out of it. Then I knew you were alive. The retainer was vibrating in my hands. If you were dead, I would have gotten nothing."

"You know, Dayle, for two days my teeth were hurting me. This is very spooky," she remarked.

"Tell me about the boy you were with, and why did I see you in dark cars."

"I am in love with this boy and we were living in and out of cars," she said. "I sensed my mother had hired a Psychic. I even told my boyfriend I bet Mom is using a Psychic to find me. How did you find me?"

"In answer to your question on how I found you, you made one mistake: you had your girlfriend call home. I tapped into your friend's voice and sensed you would be back at the shopping center. The rest is just a gift that I have."

"Some gift, Dayle. You know, till this day I *never* believed in Psychics. I thought all you people were a hoax. But you know something, I found out it's real. You really do have a gift, you know. Besides, you really spooked me out."

I said, "You know, Pollyann, that's the best compliment you could have given me."

As the family was leaving, they couldn't thank me enough. Pollyann hugged me and smiled. "I believe in you, Dayle Schear. Thank you for making me see the light."

CHAPTER 11

LIZZIE BORDEN

*Lizzie Borden took an axe
And gave her mother forty whacks
And when she was done
She gave her father forty-one*

I sat patiently on the steps of 92 Second Street, in the small town of Fall River, Massachusetts, waiting for the television cameras to roll. An elderly man passing by shouted the famous rhyme, "Lizzie Borden took an ax and gave her mother forty whacks." Within moments, as the chant grew louder, I felt angry; hostility poured out of me. He was uttering the very words Lizzie Borden had once heard.

Why was I so upset? After all, it was just a rhyme. For a split moment, I had become the *persona* of Lizzie Borden, outraged by the name calling, tired of being made fun of. Was this how Lizzie felt?

I flashed back in time. The steps I was sitting on pulsated. I glanced up at the attic where Bridget the maid had slept. To my left was the room in which Mrs. Borden was axed to death. Chills came over me. I felt the ugliness and violence of the house. My feelings were overpowering. I could barely contain myself and sit still while the cameras kept rolling.

As a child, I had heard the wild stories about Lizzie Borden. The children's rhyme stuck in my mind for many years. Lizzie Borden died in August of 1927, and my personal introduction to Lizzie was in the fall of 1992, one hundred years after the atrocious murders of her stepmother and father had taken place.

The story went as follows: in August of 1892, a cry of murder swept through the tiny town of Fall River, Massachusetts. The townspeople whispered among themselves.

Andrew J. Borden and his wife Abbie had been murdered in broad daylight in their home at 92 Second Street. The manner in which they were put to death was brutal and mysterious. The murderer had wielded an axe or something similar into the heads and bodies of the Borden couple.

When discovered, Mr. Borden lay stretched out at full length upon the sofa in his sitting room, blood trickling down his butchered head.

Upstairs in the guest chamber lay the body of Mrs. Borden. She had been changing the bedding. Her head rested in a large pool of blood as well.

In the house were Miss Lizzie Borden, youngest daughter of the slain couple, and Bridget Sullivan, sometimes known as Maggie, their only servant. Both had been within calling distance.

Lizzie Borden was the first to discover her stepmother. Lizzie later stated that she had spoken to her father only moments before, on his return from the city. After seeing him sitting comfortably on the sofa, she made her way to the barn.

The police and townspeople were baffled by this mystery. Nothing within the house had been touched or moved; robbery was ruled out. Writers and folks throughout Fall River accused Lizzie Borden of this unearthly crime.

Approximately nine months after her arrest, Lizzie Borden was acquitted at her trial. In those days, it was a rarity for a woman to be accused of and tried for a murder.

Till this day there is an endless debate about the Fall River axe murders. The crime was never solved, although detailed information can be found in many books such as *The Fall River Tragedy*.

This is where I came in. I never in my wildest imagination dreamed I would ever come face to face with Lizzie Borden or her past. I was to embark upon this adventure with mixed emotions.

My expertise as a Psychic is in psychometry. By touching an object, whether the object is one day old or one hundred years old, I receive impressions as if they were happening now. That's how my gift works.

This assignment to research Lizzie Borden's past was most unusual. Usually I'm asked to find missing people or solve a murder. However, Lizzie Borden had been dead for well over sixty-five years. Why would anyone want to stir this murder up again over one hundred years later?

I remember well the month it all began; it was July, 1992. My husband Blythe and I were making arrangements for my Honolulu trip to promote my first book, *Dare to Be Different!*, which was just about to roll off the press.

Late one evening, we were watching a new television show called *Sightings*. I noticed flying saucers across the television screen; this definitely caught my eye. We continued watching the show and were amazed at its authenticity. I decided this was a show I wanted to be on. "Blythe, please get a promotional tape ready. I want to send it out." From my past performances, Blythe knew that when I key onto a television show, I know I will be on it in the future. He wasted no time.

Within two weeks we heard from *Sightings*. A lady named Maggie called to let me know she had received my promotional tape. The producers were impressed. My conversation with Maggie lasted for about an hour. "Dayle, we'd like to film you for our show. Tell me some interesting stories that have happened to you recently," she said. I rattled on for Maggie, but she seemed to want something new, something fresh.

I explained that within the last year I had appeared on *Hard Copy* several times, and I had given that television show most of my unusual stories. Maggie listened intently, then decided to wait a while until she felt the right story for me came along. I must say my hopes were dashed to the ground as I listened to Maggie's voice; I felt I had lost my chance. I thanked her anyway for her interest.

Two long weeks pasted. One day, after running errands around town, I arrived at home and was met by an excited Blythe. "Dayle!" he shouted "*Sightings* called. They found a story for you. It's a famous case—it has something to do with an axe—that happened many years ago."

"An axe!" I responded. "The only axe I recall has to do with the Lizzie Borden case."

"That's it! Whatever you just said, the Lizzie Borden or something. That's it." Blythe could hardly contain himself.

"Blythe, are you familiar with the Lizzie Borden case?" I asked.

"No," he answered. "Who is she?"

"Blythe, the Lizzie Borden case is so famous. Where have you been?"

"Hawaii! Why?"

"The Lizzie Borden case was made into a movie starring Elizabeth Montgomery."

I explained what I remembered from history about Lizzie Borden. "This could be exciting, reaching back in time to find out what really happened to her. I can't wait."

The next day we called *Sightings* and spoke this time with someone named Joyce. I mentioned to Joyce that Blythe and I were going to L.A. for a few days. She invited us to their office to meet with the producers of the show.

Filled with curiosity and excitement, I reflected upon this adventure seriously. What would be the repercussions? What if I found out that Lizzie Borden was innocent. What if I found out Lizzie Borden was guilty? What if . . . ? I didn't want to mess with a legend, nor did I want to change history. But maybe, just maybe, I was chosen to find out the truth. After analyzing the situation, I decided to take the chance.

Blythe and I started off for L.A. We wanted to save a little money after spending so much to publish my book, so we drove. The drive humbled us. Eleven hours later we arrived in L.A.

The next day we were refreshed and ready to meet with the producers of *Sightings* in their office on Wilshire Boulevard. We were greeted at the front desk and asked to have a seat momentarily.

A pretty young lady introduced herself as Michelle and started to ramble on about her concept of the Lizzie Borden case. "Well, Dayle, we want to send you to Massachusetts. There's a museum in Fall River that houses some of Lizzie Borden's items. Why, they even have Lizzie Borden's stepmother's hair and bloodstained quilt for you to touch."

"Whoa!" I said. "How interesting."

"Dayle, this is going to be a spectacular piece. I just feel it in my bones."

Everyone else agreed. We spent several hours at the office. I slowly got to know each of the producers. I offered my services and gave them free readings. Their faces reflected both pleasure and amazement. Within a few short hours I had "won" their hearts.

Joyce said, "Dayle, give me your schedule. I'll be contacting you in a few days. Call me when you get back to Tahoe."

My schedule was hectic. I knew this trip to Fall River, Massachusetts, would squeeze right in between my trip to Hawaii. Time was crucial. The way the studio explained it to me, we were to leave for Boston by way of San Francisco on Saturday, September 19, 1992. On the 20th we would arrive at the Day's Inn in Providence, Rhode Island. Then we would pick up a rental car and drive to Fall River, just in time to film the scene in the graveyard where Lizzie Borden was buried.

However, at the last minute the studio changed the itinerary. Now, we were directed on a different course, one of a spiritual nature at that. Not even the studio knew what we were to encounter.

My new itinerary was: Blythe and I were to leave for Boston on September 19th as planned. But the studio wanted us to stay at the *Popular Inn* in Somerset, Massachusetts, a stone's throw from Fall River, instead of at the Day's Inn in Providence. That way we could film everything within two days.

We decided to make the most of our back-East trip and visit some of my relatives. I would meet my sister Terrie, who was to be in Providence while I was filming in Fall River. After the shoot, we planned to drive about four hours to my hometown in New Jersey. *But the best laid plans of mice and men often fail.*

We arrived on schedule and had very few problems finding the Popular Inn, which was tucked away in the middle of the country. The inn was over one hundred years old and beautiful. Shortly thereafter, I met with the segment producer. We discussed our itinerary over dinner and what they expected of me during the next day's shoot.

Our first shoot in the afternoon would be at the graveyard site of Lizzie Borden and family. An idea flashed before my eyes. I wanted to take a rocking chair, place it next to Lizzie Borden's grave and hold an axe. I felt part of me would become part of her. The producer agreed.

September 20th. In the afternoon we shot the scene at the graveyard. Impressions came to me rapidly. Visions of Lizzie appeared before me, as she spoke to me telepathically from the grave. I could hear her laughing ever so faintly. She told me that no one would really find out who killed her stepmother and father; I would be wasting my time. The filming lasted about an hour or so. Soon after, the producer called it a wrap.

The day was almost over. Blythe and I had time to relax as we drove to the airport. My sister's plane would be arriving in Providence at 2:30 in the afternoon. We had plenty of time to meet her. Fall River is about thirty minutes away from Providence.

I had something special for my sister. I brought along with me some pictures of her wedding, pictures she never had seen before. Terrie couldn't remember any pictures being taken at her wedding. These pictures had been given to me by my cousin Donald, whom I had persuaded to part with these special photos.

In years past, my sister and I never saw eye to eye. Little did I know these pictures would open the door for a brighter future. We looked through the photographs ever so carefully. There was my father in all his glory. My mother was so young and beautiful. Remembrance of years past flowed between us. There was a picture of me as a little girl holding a bouquet of flowers, and a special picture of Terrie and her husband Al, as they cut the wedding cake. We shared tears of joy and laughter.

For the first time that I could remember, my sister and I opened up to each other. Not only did the pictures come alive, so did we. We laughed and cried. And now, thirty-five years later, on the eve of my sister's anniversary, the timeless photographs reunited all of us. Magical pictures, they once bound my sister and brother-in-law, and now they bound my sister and me.

The evening came to a close. We kissed and hugged as we said our good-byes. Blythe and I couldn't stop talking about the magical pictures.

Later that evening, we drove back to the Popular Inn. I decided to read a little bit before retiring. As we sat in bed, I felt a coldness come over me. All the windows were closed. I glanced over at the clock on the wall; it read one o'clock in the morning. Within seconds, I heard footsteps approaching our room. The floor was creaking. I couldn't imagine who was walking toward our room. Then I felt something brush against my arm. I turned around—no one was there. I glanced toward the window. Suddenly, I ducked and pulled the covers over my head. An axe was flying at me! I screamed inwardly. Then I realized it was only my imagination. Or was it? I closed the Lizzie Borden book and went to sleep.

Bright and early, ready for the next day's shoot, Blythe and I joined the film crew at the breakfast table. Our discussion centered on the strange thing that happened to me the night before. Much to my surprise, I wasn't the only one who had heard the footsteps. So had the segment producer. We quickly dropped the subject and discussed the shoot for the day.

The shoot would be at Lizzie Borden's old house on 92 Second Street. Then we would go to the museum. We hurriedly finished our breakfast, then drove to Lizzie's house. The cameras were rolling. The producer wanted me to sit on the front steps of the house. I approached the house with caution and fear. I looked up toward the attic. An eerie feeling came over me. I felt as though there had been many murders committed in this house. I could barely contain myself and sit still. The producers asked me what I was feeling. I described my feelings: I was scared; I wanted to run and hide. We were not allowed into the house. I had to visualize what went on in the 1800s. I could feel movement in the house—murder, death, loneliness.

I found out later that Lizzie Borden's father was an undertaker who embalmed the bodies in the basement of his home. We finished shooting in front of Lizzie's old house. It was hard for me to pick up a great deal of information without being able to enter the house.

So, we left for the museum. The Lizzie Borden museum was unbelievable. I sat on the floor of the museum as the caretakers opened up the showcases. I was the first person in years who was allowed to touch Lizzie's clothing. There were numerous items that I could hold on to—a bloodstained quilt, a lock of Mr. Borden's hair, an axe. Very carefully, one by one, the items were placed in my lap. I was cautioned not to move any of the objects around. The caretakers feared that, due to the age of the items, something could happen to each object. The items were priceless.

I sat in one position as I touched each item carefully. Within moments, visions came to my mind's eye. I was no longer in the museum. Mentally, I was transported to Lizzie's house while I touched the quilt and a lock of her father's hair.

I saw Lizzie reach for an axe while her stepmother was making the bed in a different room. Lizzie came up behind her stepmother. I saw her stepmother look up over her shoulder. She started to scream. Lizzie struck her repeatedly from behind, killing her. Then Lizzie left the room as if nothing had happened. I watched as Lizzie went downstairs to wash her hands, as well as the axe. A second axe lay hidden in the basement under a concrete block. She reached for the axe and hid it under her clothing.

In my next vision, I saw her father lying peacefully in the living room. Lizzie Borden crept up to her sleeping father, just as Bridget the maid started to enter the room. Lizzie did not hear her; some sort of music was playing. Lizzie took the axe and slew her father as well. Tears ran down her cheeks. She glanced to her left and out of the corner of her eye saw Bridget. Bridget was silent. She followed Lizzie into another room and watched intently as Lizzie washed the blood stains from her clothes.

Suddenly, the vision was no more. I snapped back to reality; I was holding the clothing at the museum. I felt the anger of Lizzie Borden. Her father was cheap; he had deprived his daughter for many years. Lizzie was made fun of. She wanted money. She wanted to live as a queen, and she loathed her stepmother.

I learned later that Lizzie spent only about nine months in prison and was acquitted at her trial. She received the insurance money. Since it was a double murder, the insurance paid double (an enormous sum of money for those days).

Well, my job was over. I just relayed what I saw for the *Sightings* crew. Believe it or not, Lizzie was right. No one will ever know for sure. With my shoot for *Sightings* over, within a day I would be on my way to New Jersey.

Blythe and I made our way back to the Popular Inn. We met with Donna-Jean Walker, the owner of the Inn, and told her all about our day. I mentioned to her that I was a writer and had just completed my first book, *Dare to Be Different!* I had a few copies in my suitcase upstairs in my room; I ran to get a book for her.

While I was gone, Donna-Jean asked Blythe where I was from. He told her Lake Tahoe, and that we also spend six months a year in Hawaii. When I returned from my room and handed Donna-Jean my book, she said, "We have a doctor who lives a few houses away from us. He's from Lake Tahoe, also."

"No kidding! What's his name?" I asked.

"Dr. Plosker," she said.

"That name sounds familiar to me. Let me think for a moment."

"Dayle, he was the only O.B.-gynecologist in Lake Tahoe. You must know him," she insisted.

"Wait a minute. Oh, my god, I do know him!" I said excitedly, "Blythe, open my book to page 165. I think that's the same doctor in my book. He was the one who saved my life. You know, the doctor I wanted to thank, but I couldn't remember his name. I know that's him.

"Donna-Jean, can you call him on the phone? I want to talk to him."

Donna-Jean hesitated. "Well, I don't like to disturb the doctor at home. Besides, I think he's at the hospital," she said.

"No, Donna, if you call now, I know you can reach him."

Donna-Jean, however, waited several minutes before calling; I suppose she was trying to formulate her words. When she did call, he had just left for the hospital.

"Sorry, Dayle, I'll try to get hold of him in the morning." I hoped I would get a chance to thank the doctor before I left for New Jersey the next day. We all retired to our bedrooms. Blythe and I sat in bed, watching television. We noticed a storm was approaching the Atlantic coast. The weather was damp and musty.

I placed a call to my Aunt Mollie in New Jersey. She was down with a terrible cold. Her voice was hoarse and she could barely speak. I decided it wouldn't be a good idea to visit her this time, although my heart ached to see her. The next call I placed was to my cousin Jackie. She had taken on a new job and would be working on the days I would be in New Jersey. I gave up. Everyone I wanted to see was busy or sick except my cousin David, but he was just a little too far to visit. I gave up trying and hung up the phone.

"Blythe, I don't understand this. I guess we have to cancel our trip to New Jersey." I was disgusted. "Why is this happening to me? I just want to go home."

I called the airlines. Of course, there were no flights available to San Francisco. "I give up!" My temper began to rage. *"Why is this happening?"*

Blythe snickered. "I guess you don't understand the Universe yet, do you? Just be patient. Tomorrow is another day," he said. "I know, let's go to Vermont. I've never been to Vermont. The autumn leaves are changing. It's just beautiful there. Then at least, the trip won't be wasted."

With that very thought I fell asleep holding on to my automobile club book.

When I awoke in the morning, the first thing I did was to turn on the television. There was a hurricane approaching the Atlantic Coast, including Vermont. Here we go again. I guess I wasn't supposed to go anywhere.

I called to the studio in Los Angeles. Joyce answered the phone. "Dayle, I'm so glad to hear from you. We were hoping you didn't leave for New Jersey. We want you in L.A. for one more shoot. Can you come to L.A. within two days?" She paused. "We'll pay for everything."

I started laughing. "Joyce, you won't believe this. The reason I called was to tell you I'm stranded at the Popular Inn." I explained about my relatives and the storm approaching.

"Well!" she remarked. "Dayle, call the airlines and book a flight to L.A., then call me back."

That I did. Of course, all flights were open to L.A. Within two days Blythe and I would be in L.A. once again.

Meanwhile, back at the inn, Donna-Jean contacted Dr. Plosker, who was willing to meet with me later. This could be interesting. Blythe and I went shopping for the rest of the day. When we returned at 9:00 p.m., Lisa Paulo, a reporter from *The Spectator* in Somerset, was waiting to meet me. She wanted an interview for the local paper.

Lisa and I talked endlessly for about an hour. I mentioned the strange events involving Dr. Plosker. Donna-Jean called the doctor to come over so the reporter could meet with the two of us.

Dr. Plosker arrived within the hour, and I greeted him at the door. It only took a moment to recognize him as the doctor who saved my life. But Doctor Plosker had seen hundreds of patients since 1984. Why would he remember me?

I said to him, "Doc, to refresh your memory, I was living in Lake Tahoe. You were my doctor; in fact, you were the only O.B./Gyn in the whole town. I was pregnant and bleeding throughout my pregnancy. You were very kind to me.

"Four months into my pregnancy, I started to miscarry. I drove myself to Barton Memorial Hospital, and you were waiting there for me. I was bleeding profusely. You held my hand and told me not to worry. Shortly, thereafter, you wheeled me into surgery. Within an hour I was fine. Four days passed and I was still weak from losing so much blood. I lay in the hospital, looking out of the window. When you came to check on me, I asked you for a blood transfusion. You refused. You told me to sit there and make my own blood. I was angry."

The doctor sat patiently on the couch next to Donna-Jean and the reporter. All were listening intently.

I continued. "You told me you weren't going to give me a blood transfusion, that there was some bad blood going around, and you said I should sit there and make my own blood. You said, 'Some day you'll thank me.'"

The doctor interrupted. "That sounds like me."

"At the time I thought you were crazy," I said. "Why would a doctor let his patient suffer? It wasn't until I wrote my book, *Dare to Be Different,* that I realized how kind you were." I paused, then explained.

"The year of my miscarriage was 1984. It was also the beginning of the AIDS virus. God only knows, if you *did* give me that blood transfusion, what would have happened to me. I probably would not be here to thank you. I never knew how to find you, and I couldn't remember your name until Donna-Jean came along. I guess fate has thrown us together. I want to thank you now. Thank you, Doctor Plosker, for saving my life!"

The doctor seemed bewildered, almost as though he was trying to jar his memory. I handed him a copy of my book. When he opened it to the first chapter about Harrah's in Lake Tahoe, all at once he remembered who I was. "I remember now!" he exclaimed. His face turned bright red. I asked him what was wrong. He opened my book to the credits. "Look!" he said. "*E.S.P.* Inc. This is strange. . . ."

"Why?" I asked.

"Because my name is <u>E</u>rron <u>S</u>amuel <u>P</u>losker." I stared at him. The reporter stared at him. The doctor stared at me, and Donna-Jean stared at everyone. We shrugged our shoulders. The doctor shook his head in disbelief.

It was getting late. After we had several pictures taken together, Dr. Plosker thanked me for the book and exited quietly.

The reporter wrote a fabulous feature about the doctor and me. The article can be found in *The Spectator,* Somerset, Massachusetts September 30, 1992 issue.

Well! Now I knew why I was meant to stay in Somerset. We thanked Donna-Jean and her husband, Carl, for their hospitality. I'm sure we will go back there again.

The next day, Blythe and I flew to Los Angeles. We filmed the rest of my *Sightings* segment on the Paramount lot.

We arrived home in Tahoe only to pack our things for our Hawaii trip, which would be soon.

That week I received a phone call from Somerset. Lisa, the reporter, was on the line; she wanted to let me know when the article would be out.

"By the way, Dayle, I have some information for you," she said. "I found out through another reporter that in 1984, shortly after Doctor Plosker left Lake Tahoe, he treated a patient in Somerset for a miscarriage. She was bleeding profusely. He had no choice but to give her a blood transfusion. He had to save her life. He also warned her of bad blood. This was something that stayed in her mind for many years to come. She just found out that she has the AIDS virus."

I was stunned. "Lisa, that's mind boggling. It could have been me. I'm sorry for the girl, but I know the doctor did the best he could at the time. I hope I gave him some encouragement. It must be rough on him. Someone thanks him for saving her life, while another patient is dying of AIDS."

After all was said and done, when *Sightings* aired, our three-day shoot went down the drain. All that was left of what I had shot was about five minutes of air time. It seems they had to scrap another segment and used the Lizzie Borden piece just to fill in time.

I thought about this trip for many weeks. I gradually realized the television show was just a catalyst for other events. I was meant to go to Boston to meet my sister, so we could be united once again. And above all I was meant to meet Doctor Plosker, to thank him for saving my life.

CHAPTER 12

THE CASE OF DIANE SUZUKI

Missing Since July 6, 1985

> The amazing events that led to this story are simply mind-boggling. I will give you detailed accounts of psychic impressions that were proven six years after Diane Suzuki's murder. Included is information never before released to the public. I hope this will prove without a doubt that Psychics can help law enforcement agencies.

The year 1991 was extremely memorable for me; I was interviewed on a regular basis about the Diane Suzuki case.

Early one afternoon, I received a message telling me to call a telephone number in the Los Angeles area. When I did, much to my surprise, I was connected to one of the producers of the nationally syndicated television show, *Hard Copy*. "Hi, my name is Ann. Can I help you?" she said.

"Yes, my name is Dayle Schear. I'm calling you from Hawaii. I was told someone wanted to get in touch with me."

"Yes, Ms. Schear. Our executive producer was vacationing in Hawaii; he read the article in *The Honolulu Advertiser* about your involvement in the Diane Suzuki case."

"Which article are you referring to?" I asked. "There have been so many articles written lately."

"Let me see. Here, I have it my file; here it is: 'Police Search Marsh Close To Suspect's Home.' After reading the article, my producer felt you were getting a bum deal. Detectives all over the mainland use Psychics. Why isn't the Honolulu police department giving you credit?" she asked.

"Well, it's a long story. I feel I gave the police several clues. However, they don't believe in Psychics. There's nothing I can do," I replied.

"We'd like to send a crew into Hawaii to cover the story. The only problem is, no one will speak to us. We gather there's a cover-up," she stated.

I assured her there wasn't a cover-up of any kind. "The island people believe they must take care of their own. They don't like outsiders. They probably feel *Hard Copy* will do them more harm than good," I said. "Even though the police department doesn't like Psychics, it's okay; the people of the island believe in me, and that's all that matters. I can't do your story; I live on the island, and I respect the people's wishes. Do you understand?"

"Yes, I understand your feelings," Ann responded. "But my producer is not going to like this. I'll have to check with him and see what he says. You may not have a choice. The story will be written with you or without you. I'll call you in a few days and let you know what happens."

I thought momentarily, if everyone refuses to speak to *Hard Copy,* they can't possibly get a story. I was determined to keep my mouth shut. Several days passed and I heard nothing. But within a week *Hard Copy* called me once again; they had a reporter on a plane headed for Hawaii, and could I please meet him at the Ilikai Hotel at 6:00 p.m. If I would just talk to him, they wouldn't press me for a story.

My husband Blythe and I decided to meet the reporter from *Hard Copy*. When we arrived at the Ilikai on time, he was waiting for us. His name was Doug Bruckner, a handsome, personable fellow in his forties with salt-and-pepper hair. Doug greeted us and asked us to join him for dinner.

Over dinner, he laid out his purpose for meeting with me. "Dayle, I came here to do a story on Diane Suzuki. We want to portray the girl with the utmost respect. We have no intentions of police bashing; we just want to report the facts about the girl."

"I understand, Doug. I don't want to be on national television. I enjoy being a Psychic based in Hawaii. You can ruin everything I've built up if you write this story in a negative way. I can't let that happen."

He said, "Dayle, many years ago I was a TV reporter in the islands. I understand the people. There must be a cover-up. The police won't talk to me. The family won't talk. And now you won't talk. We want to catch her killer as well as you do. Please believe me; I will write a heartwarming story about Diane Suzuki."

"I don't know," I stated, shaking my head. I felt backed into a corner.

"Dayle, I was sent here to do a story. I have to write it one way or another. If you don't cooperate, I'll have to trash the police and everyone else. I really don't want to do this. Please help us."

I paused to gather my thoughts. "I guess I don't have a choice. Can I oversee what you write? If so, I'll do it. I don't want the Suzuki family trashed or the police trashed."

"You got it!" he said. "Can we start now? I want to hear everything about Diane Suzuki."

"I have to pick up my niece at the airport; she's flying in to Hawaii within the hour."

"Can I help you?" he asked.

"Okay, we could use the help," I responded. My niece is bringing a lot of luggage. She'll be staying with me for a while. Then I'm leaving for Lake Tahoe to write my book, *Dare to Be Different*. We can talk on the way to the airport."

We arrived at the airport just in time to pick up my niece, Jackie. I introduced Jackie to Doug.

Jackie made a point to pull me aside. "Aunt Dayle, I know that man; he covered Jeff's death in L.A." Jeff was my nephew, who had died suddenly on the doctor's table after having a simple nose operation. Foul play was suspected. I found out through Jackie that Doug had written a great story on Jeff. That was all I needed to hear. I knew Doug would be fair.

At my home in Hawaii Kai, Doug was all ears.

"Okay, Dayle, why don't you start at the beginning with how you got involved in the Diane Suzuki case. I won't interrupt you, unless I don't understand something. Wait just one minute while I turn on the tape recorder."

"Doug, this is a long story. My involvement in the Diane Suzuki case spans well over five years."

Doug responded, "I have plenty of time; don't worry. Just start at the beginning." Doug snuggled in, nice and comfy, as if this were going to be a long night. Everyone else sat around the table in anticipation.

This is the story as I related it to Doug.

Day 1. It all started on July 6th, to be exact. Blythe and I were vacationing on the island of Maui. We had no knowledge of the Diane Suzuki case until we arrived home.

My phone rang. Blythe answered and took down all the pertinent information. "Dayle, don't bother to unpack your things. We have to head to Aiea. A young lady by the name of Diane Suzuki is missing. Her sister Susan just called. The police are organizing a massive search party."

I grabbed my purse and off we went to Aiea. When we arrived at the Suzuki family home, the press was all over the place. I ducked in; I didn't want to be noticed. I sat down with Susan Suzuki and Diane's best friend, Cora.

Susan exclaimed, "My sister is missing! I've heard you have an excellent record for finding missing people. Diane was last seen at the Rosalie Woodson Dance school in Aiea, teaching her routine dance class. By the way, I don't want my parents to know that I've hired a Psychic. I don't want them to be upset with your findings. They can barely deal with the police and the media. I don't mean to hurt your feelings, but you understand, don't you?"

I replied, "Yes, I do, Susan. I ask only one thing: please don't release my name to the press. My life could be in danger."

I asked for clothing of Diane's; I wanted to do a reading in her home. We walked into her bedroom. I sat down, holding on to Diane's clothing, slowly receiving impressions, which I recorded into my tape recorder. Then I made my way to Diane's car and sat with her best friend, Cora. I grabbed the steering wheel of the car slowly. I closed my eyes tightly; visions of Diane appeared before my closed eyes.

"Oh, my God, there's a struggle; I see a struggle! I see her trying to get loose from a young man. Now I see Diane out of this car. I see the young man holding her hands behind her back."

Cora interjected, "Dayle, you're right. What you're seeing happened last week. Diane and her boyfriend got into a fight. He slapped her around a little bit."

"A little bit!" I exclaimed. "Are you sure, Cora?"

"Yes, I'm sure. Diane told me about this last week."

"Okay, I know I'm on the right track now. You see, sometimes it's hard to know what time frame I'm in. This gives me a good idea; I'm about a week in the past." I suggested we go to the dance studio, since that was the last place Diane was seen alive. I asked Susan, "Do you have any recent pictures of Diane?"

"Yes," she responded. "But there is a roll of film that hasn't been developed yet. Wait, the photographer from the school took pictures of Diane; I'll see if I can get hold of them. Why don't you, Cora and Blythe go to the dance school. I'll try to retrieve the pictures."

"Susan, the pictures are very important for me to do my work. The pictures could be the key to everything," I remarked.

"I understand. I'll hurry."

We went to the dance studio, which was about ten minutes from Diane Suzuki's home. While we were driving, Cora felt compelled to tell me about the case.

"Dayle, I feel like it's all my fault."

"What do you mean, Cora?"

"Well, if it wasn't for me, Diane wouldn't have disappeared. You see, after her dance class, we were getting ready to go to Turtle Bay Hilton. I was downstairs waiting for her, but . . . but . . . I fell asleep. I was tired. Usually I wait in the dance room for her. When I awoke, I looked at my watch; it was about 3:15 p.m. I hurried and ran upstairs to get Diane—I didn't want to miss her. Her purse was there, but she was gone. I searched all over the dance studio. She was nowhere to be found. I never should have fallen asleep."

"Cora, don't blame yourself. There's nothing you could have done. Trust me on this one," I said.

When we arrived at the dance studio, we climbed the stairs, endlessly, to the top. There was a long corridor leading to the entrance of the dance studio. The cops and press were swarming all over the place. I made myself invisible once again. Cora pointed to where Diane was last seen.

Back in the storage area of the dance studio was a bathroom, which had not been used in a while; it seemed to be out of order. I was picking up strange feelings around this area. I walked out of the bathroom, turned to my right and walked about three feet to an area with a lot of boxes. I stopped.

"You see, Doug, there was a fifteen-minute span in which Diane Suzuki disappeared from the face of the earth. At 3:00 p.m., she was seen in the dance studio; at 3:15 p.m., she was missing. News reports said that Diane was last seen talking to someone outside of the dance studio. In fact, in the beginning, the police believed she got into a car with someone she knew.

"Doug, this case was bewildering."

Doug nodded. "Go on, Dayle, I want to hear more."

After I walked through the rest of the studio, I asked Blythe if we could trace the route by car from the dance studio to Diane Suzuki's house.

When we arrived at Diane's house, Susan gave me some of Diane's belongings to take home and sleep with. It was time to go.

I needed some peace and quiet. I told Cora and Susan I would be back tomorrow afternoon.

Blythe and I didn't go right home; we kept circling the house. We drove to the school, then to Aloha Stadium. I turned to Blythe and said, "There's something in that school for me; I don't know what it is. I feel she never left the school." I paused, knowingly but confused. Part of me believed she left with a friend. The other part of me knew she never left the school alive. I was perplexed.

Blythe said, "Let's go home, Dayle. Why don't you hold her clothing on your lap and see what impressions you get."

I asked Blythe to keep driving for a while. I was being pulled toward the Aloha Stadium once again. We circled the stadium endlessly. Then a feeling came over me while I was holding her clothes. I was pulled back to her house and then to her school. Something inside of me felt she was still in the school. Or maybe she left something behind. I couldn't shake the feeling.

Night was approaching. Blythe and I headed home reluctantly. That evening I slept with Diane's clothing.

Day 2. Before heading for Aiea I made a phone call to Lt. Haig Kalauokalani of the Kailua police department. We had been friends for years. I explained my involvement with the Diane Suzuki case and asked him if he would join me in Aiea that afternoon. I somehow wanted protection. I didn't know why; I just wanted him with me.

"Dayle, you realize that's out of my jurisdiction, but . . . ," He paused. "It's my day off. I can go with you undercover. I'll tell you what; I'll meet you at the dance studio within the hour."

I looked at my watch; it was 1:30. When Blythe and I arrived at the studio, we didn't have to wait long; Lt. Haig pulled up right beside us. We took him for a ride from the dance studio to Diane's house, where we picked up Cora, then back to the studio.

I felt restless. "Haig, there's something in that studio."

"Why don't we go upstairs and find out what's bothering you," he said.

I was cautious. "But the place is swarming with police and media."

"Don't worry, Dayle, you're with me. Just do your thing."

Blythe, Cora, Haig and I walked up the stairs toward the dance studio, ducking away from police and media. I started walking past the bathroom in the storage area. We came to a dead end fast; we were surrounded by boxes all over the place.

"Haig," I shouted, "I smell death! Can you smell what I smell? It smells like a dead body."

"Dayle, it smells like cleaning solution," he said. Haig checked around. The room had been cleaned from top to bottom with some sort of cleaning solution.

"That doesn't matter; I smell a death," I insisted. I stood alone, spacing out momentarily. To the right of me, no more than a few feet away, stood Blythe, Haig and Cora in deep conversation.

I glanced down at the studio floor, which was covered with dust. Noticing a shiny object lying on the floor, I bent down to pick it up. It was a gold pendant with the initial "D" and a tiny diamond attached above it.

"Oh my God, this is Diane's pendant; I know it is." I looked it over from top to bottom. It had blood on it. As I held the pendant tightly in my hand, I realized she'd never left the studio alive. She was dead.

"Blythe, Haig, Cora. Come over here. Cora, do you recognize this pendant?"

Cora exclaimed, "I think it's Diane's. I saw her wearing the pendant the day she was teaching class. She never takes that pendant off. I think it's hers!"

"Haig, what should I do?" I asked. "There's a detective over there talking to the press. I want to give him the pendant."

Haig didn't think that was a good idea. "Dayle, you can't interrupt him. Besides, if you give him the pendant, that will be the end of it. Why don't you take the pendant home and do a reading on it. Then call the police and tell them how you found it."

Reluctantly, I listened. I still wanted to do the right thing. I waited for what seemed an eternity to get the detective's attention, but he was still talking to the press. I finally decided to leave. We drove to Diane's house. Susan was there.

"Well, did you guys come up with anything?" she asked.

"Yes! I found this pendant. I need to confirm it's Diane's," I said.

Susan took the pendant and asked the other family members. No one was positive that the pendant belonged to Diane.

As fate would have it, the studio pictures I asked for the day before arrived while I was holding the pendant in my hand. We looked through the photos carefully. There was a picture of Diane Suzuki, wearing a pendant with the initial "D" around her neck.

Amazing! We all stared at each other. I knew now that Diane wanted me to find her pendant, so I could put together the pieces of the puzzle.

Haig shouted, "Dayle, take the pendant home! Hurry!"

I looked up at Susan and asked if I could take the studio pictures home with me.

"Yes," she said.

While driving home, I held the pictures in my hand, along with her pendant.

"Blythe! Oh my God!"

"What's the matter?" he said.

"I know who killed Diane!"

"Who?"

"It's a young man. He works for the dance studio. I see him. She's struggling to get loose of him." The vision faded.

By the time we arrived home, I was drained. I waited several hours before I picked up the pendant again. I turned on my tape recorder and started a reading on Diane Suzuki.

"She's dead, Blythe. She died in the storage area. There was a young man with her. There was a struggle. She was in a hurry to leave. The young man wanted her help. He also wanted her sexually. Diane refused to help him. There were words; Diane called him names. The young man freaked out. He hit her.

"Then a blow to the head. Diane was knocked unconscious. She's not dead yet. She seems to be semiconscious.

"The next thing I see is a car. There are two or three people in the car. Diane is in the trunk. The people are driving the car all over the place. That's all I can see."

"Dayle, I think we'd better call the police," Blythe remarked.

Several hours passed before the police called me back. The conversation with a detective went as follows:

"Can I help you, Ms. Schear?"

"Yes, I think I have something of Diane Suzuki that you want."

"Oh, you do. What could you possibly have of Diane that we want?

"I have her pendant."

"Where did you get her pendant?"

"I found it in the storage room of the dance studio this afternoon."

The detective's voice suddenly had an edge to it. "What! That's impossible. I had my men on the floor of the dance studio for over four hours yesterday. We searched that room from top to bottom. It's impossible. I want you to bring that pendant down to the dance studio now," he ordered.

"But it's almost twelve midnight," I protested.

"I don't care! You'd better get down here, or I'll arrest you for taking evidence from the scene of a crime."

So Blythe and I got in the car and drove to the dance studio. There we were met by several police officers and detectives. I handed the pendant over to the detective.

"Ms. Schear, I want you to show us where you found this pendant," he said.

I walked over to the storage area and pointed to the ground.

The detective was suspicious. "I'm sorry, I just can't believe you found the pendant. My men were searching all day for any clue, and you just walk in this room on a hunch, bend down and find a pendant. Where is the chain that goes along with the pendant?"

"I don't know. I just found the pendant," I said.

Within moments, a photographer was taking pictures of the pendant on the floor exactly where I found it.

"What do you think happened to Diane?" the detective asked me.

"I think she was murdered right here in the spot where I found the pendant." There was silence.

I was told to keep my mouth shut about the pendant. The detectives didn't want anyone to know that I found the pendant.

Why, a Psychic had found the only bit of evidence connected to this case; the police could never live this down. The detective started arguing with Blythe. Again he remarked there was no way we could have found the pendant.

The detective shouted, "I wouldn't leave town if I were you! We just may want to bring you in for questioning."

Blythe was angry. He started to shout. "You know, you people drag us down here in the middle of the night; we comply, then you jump all over us. We were hired by Susan Suzuki to do a job. My wife and I haven't slept. We've been working around the clock to help solve this case. I really don't think we deserve this. I'm sorry you have problems with my wife finding the pendant. Why don't you give her a lie detector test?"

"I think we will!" The detective growled. "Remember, don't leave town!"

It was now one o'clock in the morning. Blythe and I left for home. I couldn't believe we had to go through this. It was something right out of a movie: "Don't leave town," he said.

Doug interjected, "Well, did he give you a lie detector test?"

"Yes, they did. They gave me a polygraph test *five years* later."

"My, they work fast, don't they?" Doug chuckled. "Go on with the story, Dayle; this is getting interesting." Doug was all ears.

"Oh, by the way, Doug," I said, "I did tell two people about the pendant. They were Perry and Price of KSSK radio. I told Michael and Larry everything so that I would be protected."

Day 3. I was beginning to put the pieces of the puzzle together now. I called Susan Suzuki and asked her if I could possibly meet with a detective who was open to Psychics.

That evening I was introduced to Lt. Isabelo. We met in Aiea and we talked.

"Lieutenant, I think I know who murdered Diane Suzuki."

"Why do you say murder?" he responded.

"Well! This is what I feel happened. You see, there was an argument in the dance studio. Diane was in a hurry to leave to get to the Turtle Bay Hilton. She didn't have time to talk to the young man who was bothering her, nor did she have time to help him. I feel the young man, who worked there, freaked out about something she said.

"When I held Diane's pendant, visions appeared before my eyes. I saw a young man striking her. There was a blow to her head. She was knocked unconscious. *This was an accident on his part. I don't believe he meant to hurt her in any way.* Later that evening, her body was left in the bathroom. Since no one uses the bathroom, it was safe to store her body there.

"Now keep in mind this young man is mental, not all there. I feel he couldn't handle the situation. He needed help to move the body out of the dance studio; therefore, I believe his family helped him in some way."

Lt. Isabelo stared at me for a moment. Then he opened a file that was on his lap. He showed me they had taken in a young man for a polygraph test—the same man I suspected.

When the young man in question was taken into the police station, he had scratch marks on his body, which the police photographed. When asked where the scratches came from, he said, "I was climbing under a chicken-wire fence and I got all scratched up yesterday."

He couldn't account for his whereabouts on the day or night Diane Suzuki turned up missing. He claimed he was in the back room and had scissors in his hand when he tripped and fell with a loud thump; that's how he cut himself.

Then he went into the bathroom to wash the blood off his hands. When he came out of the bathroom, he told the police, Diane had left the dance studio. That was the last time he saw her.

Lt. Isabelo pointed out that there was a dance class in the next room; yet no one heard the thump. Lt. Isabelo also stated that when the young man was given a polygraph test, it showed he was deceptive.

I touched the piece of paper with his handwriting on it; I knew he was connected with the murder. I asked Isabelo why they didn't arrest him.

"No body, no evidence. It's all circumstantial, Dayle," he said. "We have to find the body. Do you have any clues where the body can be found?"

I replied, "All I know is the body is buried. For all I know, the body could be in the young man's backyard. By the way, Lieutenant, did you get a search warrant to enter the young man's house?"

"Yes, we did. We found a shirt with blood all over it," he said.

"Lieutenant, my Psychic ability tells me, if you get another search warrant, you might find more. I know the guy is into porno. You'll find porno magazines all over the place. And he's messy. If I were you, I'd go through that house with a fine tooth comb."

That week the lieutenant searched the young man's house again and found many of the items that I told him about, such as porno magazines.

"Dayle, the latest information we have been receiving are reports that Diane got in a car with someone she knew. We now suspect there was someone else is involved. We have to pursue the car that someone spotted her in," he said.

"Lieutenant, in the beginning of this case I believed Diane got into a car with someone she knew. But after touching her pendant and pictures, I believe differently. It's an eighty-five percent chance that this young man who works at the dance studio did it." The lieutenant and I decided to keep in touch; if either of us came up with additional information, we would let the other know.

Day 4. I decided to get in touch with Lt. Haig once again. "Haig, this is Dayle Schear. Do you think we can go to the suspected murderer's house? I need to know without a doubt that this guy did it."

Haig responded, "What a wild request! You would do that?"

"Yes, I would. I'll make up a story, but I have to touch him. I need to touch him.

"Okay, I'm game. I'll go with you and Blythe. Meet you in Aiea within the hour."

Meanwhile, the stories circulating about Diane Suzuki were sending the police on wild goose chases all over town. One minute she was kidnapped. The next minute she was locked up somewhere in someone's home.

Blythe and I met Lt. Haig in Aiea and we discussed the matter as we sat in Haig's car.

"How am I going to do this?" I wondered aloud. "I know. I'll pretend I'm selling something and knock on the door." I was getting nervous. "What if he recognizes me? Maybe this isn't a good idea after all." But I thought to myself that since I was dressed rather casually, the chances of his recognizing me were slim. Besides, I could always deny who I was.

Haig said, "Don't chicken out now, Dayle. Pretend you're selling a membership to a local gym or something."

I held my breath for a dramatic moment. "Okay, here I go. If I'm not back in a few minutes, come get me."

I got out of the car slowly and approached the suspect's house. It was around 2:00 p.m. I was lucky; there was a young man raking the yard. I approached him cautiously. "Hi, my name is Barbara," I said. "Are you the man of the house?"

The young man answered, "Yes."

"Would you be interested in joining our new gym in Aiea? I have discount coupons if you're interested." I was standing about a foot from him. I was trying to pick up whatever I could via ESP, but nothing was coming through.

"No," he responded.

I tried to sound like a salesperson. "Why not? You look like you're in good shape. These coupons will give you several weeks of training and free use of our exercise equipment."

"No, I don't think so," he said. "Besides, I hurt my hand the other day."

He held out the palm of his hand to me and showed me the hole in his hand. It was the size of a fingernail mark, almost as if someone had dug a fingernail into his palm. Maybe Diane did just that in her struggle to get away. I reached out and grabbed his hand as if I were trying to soothe him. "I'm sorry about your hand," I said.

He abruptly pulled his hand away from mine. "I don't want to join a gym," he said.

"Sorry for bothering you." I turned and walked away slowly. He was beginning to suspect something.

Haig and Blythe were waiting anxiously for me in the car, which was parked several yards away from the young man's house.

I said, "Let's get out of here." We drove to a nearby restaurant.

"Well, what do you think? Did he do it?" Haig asked.

"I don't know," I replied. "When I touched him, I felt nothing. I don't know what that means. It's as if he has no future." I paused, then asked, "Can we go back to the school for a few minutes? I need to pick up some more information from the school." I was obsessed with the dance studio. I felt Diane's soul was still there.

We drove to the school and went upstairs. A girl stood in the hallway talking to someone. The moment I passed her, I felt *death* all over.

"Blythe, find out who that girl is. I have to know," I said urgently.

Blythe returned moments later with a startling piece of news. "Dayle, you're not going to believe this. The girl is the young man's sister. She teaches a class here as well."

I closed my eyes for a moment. "Now I understand. It's the sister who helped dispose of the body; it's her." I was receiving a violent reaction to the young man's sister.

As a Psychic, I know it's impossible to read "mental" persons. Sometimes they have more than one personality, and you never know which personality you're reading. That's why, when I touched the young man's hand, I saw nothing. A "mental" person's brain waves are not the same as a normal person's.

So, when I passed by his sister, all flashed before my eyes. I was able to read *his* thoughts and actions through his sister. He must have knocked Diane unconscious, and the sister helped finish her off.

"That's it; I know that's it! The sister was definitely involved," I said. "We can go home now. I have to put the pieces of the puzzle together for Susan."

Day 5. I sat in my living room and recorded a tape for Susan Suzuki. Later in the afternoon I would personally deliver the tape to her and give her my findings.

We arrived at the Suzuki family's home around three o'clock. Susan, Cora and friends were waiting. I said, "Susan, I came here to give you my findings about Diane. In the beginning of this case, I got caught up in the rush. Through telepathy, picking up the thoughts of everyone who was working on the case, I thought she was kidnapped as well. But my findings are as follows: there's a ninety percent chance she is dead. I believe the young man who works for the dance studio *killed her by accident.* I believe his sister played a large part in this. I feel she was covering up for her brother. The whole family may be involved. The young man is mental; he's not all there. It's one big cover-up.

"Diane was in the wrong place at the wrong time. The young man wanted Diane to help him do something. Diane refused, for she was in a hurry. She snapped at him. He couldn't stand rejection or anyone yelling at him. I believe he slapped her, then hit her over the head to keep her quiet.

"Diane was knocked out. He thought she was dead. I don't believe she died right away. He hid her in the bathroom till everyone left the school.

"Then he went and got his sister. At that point the sister had to make a decision whether to call the police or cover up the situation. She chose the latter. I don't know where they put the body at this time, but I'll keep looking.

"I confirmed some of my findings with Lt. Isabelo. The young man in question was brought into the police station. After extensive questioning and undergoing a polygraph test, the findings showed he was *deceptive.*

"I asked the lieutenant if they would bring his sister in for questioning. The police were more than ready to bring her in; however, his sister refused. In fact, she's already hired an attorney.

"I'm sorry, Susan. Here's the tape. Everything I've told you is on it. I believe the body is so well hidden that it will take a miracle to find her."

Susan and Cora stared at me teary-eyed. "But, Dayle, there are new reports out that Diane has been kidnapped," Susan said.

"I know, Susan, that this is hard to believe, but I trust my own ability."

"Dayle, please don't tell my mother or father. They want to believe Diane is alive," she pleaded.

"I won't, I promise. I still will continue to look for the body. I'm sorry."

Several months passed. Diane never turned up. The police were receiving calls from people all over the island. Some said she was kidnapped; others claimed she was spotted in different areas of the island. There was an intensive search for her. Her body was never found.

I searched for many years trying to locate the body of Diane Suzuki. Blythe and I devoted a lot of energy and time to this case. Year after year I was always drawn back to the dance school or the stadium, for some odd reason. I believe Diane's soul is still within the dance studio walls, waiting for someone to find her body. We keep trying periodically to locate her. Sometimes it feels like I'm looking for a needle in a haystack. It wasn't until 1991 that I sensed where her body could be.

"This is where you came in, Doug."

Doug perked up.

About six years after the incident, the police used Luminol in the dance studio bathroom. Luminol makes the blood luminescent, even if it's years old and scrubbed away. In this case, the Luminol revealed a great amount of blood on the floor and in the bathroom. Based on these tests, police concluded Suzuki had been murdered.

After six long years they reclassified the Diane Suzuki case from "missing person" to "murder." They sent the new blood samples to the mainland for analysis.

The Voice of Radio Changed My Life

The next day I received a phone call from Michael W. Perry and Larry Price of KSSK Radio. The conversation went as follows:

"Dayle, wake up. This is Michael."

"Yeah, Michael, what is it?"

"Wake up! You were right; the police found a lot of blood in the dance studio, just like you told me *six* years ago," he said.

"I know about the blood being found," I remarked sleepily.

"I think it's time we tell the public that you found the pendant," Michael suggested.

"I don't know; we could be opening up a can of worms," I said.

Michael was insistent. "Dayle, I'm putting you on the air. You were right; you knew from the beginning."

Michael asked me questions on the air about the pendant and how I found it. That's when my whole life changed.

The press were all over me. The police never confirmed or denied that I had found Diane Suzuki's pendant. The next thing I knew, Lt. Isabelo was calling me on the phone and asking me to take a polygraph test. It was *six years* after the fact and they wanted me to take a lie detector test. I said, "Of course, this might be fun."

I asked if I could bring my camera crew down to the police station and film everything. There were no objections. Never for one moment did it ever cross my mind that I just might fail the test and be made a fool of. I flew my attorney in to make sure all the questions were in order. I was more than prepared to take the test.

I had been under the impression that a lie-detector test would take only a few minutes. This test lasted four hours. I was nervous, but the examiner was experienced and calmed me down. He wired me up; it felt like I was attached to one big blood pressure machine. The thought crossed my mind: is this how they electrocute a person?

I noticed the examiner was asking me the same questions over and over again, sometimes by rewording them. I was getting bored. I knew I wasn't going to change my answers, but maybe this was how they break down a criminal. What an experience, but I must admit I did enjoy it. I'm probably one of the very few people who liked taking a lie-detector test. Of course, if one is lying, it must feel like hell. Four hours later, I emerged from the little room a winner; I had passed with flying colors.

News briefs started breaking every few hours on the Diane Suzuki case. The Honolulu police were sending the blood samples to the mainland. Things were stirring up.

I decided this would be a good time to go back to the suspect's house, so we circled the block and came upon a marshlike area that drew my attention. I had very disturbing feelings about this area. I felt that someone could have buried a body in this spot.

When I arrived home, I called Lt. Isabelo and explained the feelings I had upon arriving at the marsh near the young man's house.

"Are you sure, Dayle?" he asked.

"I'm sure. You know that's private property; I don't know if we can get a permit to dig. Maybe we can try."

I explained to the lieutenant that I was going to do my television show and mention the Diane Suzuki case. I also explained that I would devote some time talking about what it felt like to take a lie-detector test.

The lieutenant paused before saying, "Is that all?"

"Yes," I responded.

"Don't you want to do a little more than that?" he asked.

I gathered the lieutenant wanted me to shake the case up a bit. Not a bad idea, I thought. Then I decided to bring Diane's clothing with me down to the studio and do a reading on the air. Maybe some new information would emerge.

The night of my television show I was nervous. Even I didn't know what I was going to say. During the reading, the words came flowing out of my mouth mechanically, almost as if I had lost control. My body was vibrating at an incredible frequency. I felt like someone or something was going through me.

According to the transcript from my television show, *ESP & YOU,* this is what I said as I held Diane's clothing on my lap:

"Diane Suzuki is dead. She died in the dance studio. She was murdered. Diane was murdered by someone she knew. Someone who worked in the dance studio.

"There was a blow to her head. She struggled. This was a cover-up. Two or three people were involved with her burial. The man who killed her meant her no harm. It was an accident. It was an accident.

"Her body is in one place and her clothing is in another place. I see a marshlike area where the clothes or body might be. Whoever did this, you must confess. You must confess."

No sooner did these words come out of my mouth than I snapped out of my trancelike state. It took me well over twenty minutes to recover. I had no knowledge of what I had said until I viewed the tape later that evening. My director, Mark Williams, was astounded with the footage he got.

"Dayle, I swear that wasn't you talking. Come in the control room and look at this tape with me. It's amazing. See for yourself."

I stared at the footage. "It looks like me. It sounds like me. But it isn't me. I mean it is, but it isn't. This is hard to explain. I look like I'm in a trance."

Mark remarked, "You sure do."

ESP & YOU aired several hours later. Most of Hawaii must have been watching, for the ratings were incredible.

Several days passed. I turned on the six o'clock news as usual and there, much to my surprise, was Lieutenant Dias, being interviewed. The police were filmed digging up a small portion of the Waiau marsh, the same marsh I had described on my television show. The police retrieved some tights and clothing out of the marsh.

When Lieutenant Dias was asked, "Does this have anything to do with Dayle Schear and her television show?" His stuttering response, live on television, was, "The timing of the search had nothing to do with Schear's program on Wednesday."

Surprised, shocked, I stood there watching Lt. Dias. "I can't believe this man is saying I had nothing to do with his search. Someone ought to give him a lie-detector test," I chuckled.

The response of the public was that of outrage. I personally received several hundred calls that week from viewers, most of whom couldn't believe that Lt. Dias denied everything.

I was fed up. The Suzuki family *never once* thanked me for helping them. The police denied my very existence. *Déjà vu,* this incident reminded me of the "Roxanne Tandal" case.

In that particular case I had directed the family to where the body would be found. There was an arrest, and, when we were ready to go to press, the story was axed by officials in the police department, or so I was told by one of the reporters. When will it end, this persecution of Psychics?

This article ran in the *Washington Times,* shortly after my television show and polygraph test:

> **Pendant Power**
>
> By Diane Keating 7/25/91
>
> Police sometimes disregard psychic-supplied information that later turns out to be correct.
>
> Within days of the 1985 disappearance of 19-year-old Diane Suzuki, who vanished from the Oahu, Hawaii, dance studio where she had been teaching a class, family members called in Honolulu psychic Dayle Schear.
>
> "In the first few days when I was checking it out," Ms. Schear says, "I asked the family for recent pictures of Diane. They said a photographer had some undeveloped pictures. Later, I went to the school, where I felt I would find something of hers.
>
> "In a storage room I found a tiny gold pendant with the initial 'D' and having a small diamond. Her family was not sure it was hers, but when the pictures came back, she was wearing that same pendant."
>
> Ms. Schear says she used psychometry on both the pendant and the photographs to divine that the young woman had been

murdered in the storage room. But when the psychic told police about finding Diane Suzuki's pendant, they suggested she had planted it.

Now six years after her disappearance, new evidence suggests Miss Suzuki was killed in the storage room. In recent days police have been digging up a watercress field where Ms. Schear earlier had said the girl's body would be found. Last week searchers unearthed a pair of tights believed to be Miss Suzuki's.

I was overwhelmed by the press; articles were appearing everywhere on television and in the newspapers. This was the first time the Diane Suzuki story gained national attention.

The *Washington Times* reporter couldn't understand why no one had listened to me six years ago. Now I was faced with *Hard Copy* wanting to make a hero of me, when all I did was find a pendant and discover a murder. I felt demoralized.

It was time to get out of the islands for a while and go back to the mainland. I wanted to write my book, *Dare to Be Different!*, and become a lot less visible.

"Doug, that's the story in a nutshell," I said.

"Well, Dayle, this explains why the police don't want to talk to me either. The Suzuki family must be listening to the detectives. I'm still going to write this story, no matter how hard they make it for me. We'll start filming tomorrow, he said. "Thanks for sharing your story with me. It's getting late. I'll see you tomorrow"

"Doug, before you leave. . . ."

"Yes?"

"Remember, you promised not to bash the police. I still feel they were up against a lot of pressure. I know Lt. Isabelo did a good job. Please write a nice story on Diane," I pleaded.

"You know, Doug," I continued, "in my heart I believe Lt. Isabelo knew all along who killed Diane Suzuki. I think the police never made an arrest because they felt there wasn't enough evidence. I know and Isabelo knows there was more than enough evidence to warrant an arrest and convict this young man, even without a body. I feel Isabelo wasn't in the position to make an arrest, but if it were up to him, he would have.

"I feel badly for the Suzuki family. They wanted so badly to believe their daughter was alive. Till this day, no matter what anyone says, they still have hope that someday Diane will be walking through their door," I said.

"There comes a time in one's life where you have to let go of dreams and face reality. I hope someday Susan and her family will face this situation and press hard for an arrest. If they don't, all will be lost; Diane will have died in vain, with her killer gone free. It's time they stand up and fight, not turn the other cheek. Till this day, almost everyone knows who the murderer of Diane Suzuki is. The case now lies on the D.A.'s desk, pending. Till someone fights or makes a fuss, that's where it will stay."

"I get your point," Doug said. "Maybe our story will help them see the light. Dayle, remember, you are the only person talking to us, and besides some old footage, I have nothing. I'll do my best. By the way, the studio wants to pay you for your trouble."

"No, Doug, I want nothing. Thanks, anyway."

The filming took about a week. I don't know how Doug did it, but he did. Everything went smoothly. He mentioned the show would air sometime in the fall. The funny thing was, the show would air everywhere except in Hawaii, because the affiliate station in Honolulu had dropped *Hard Copy* from its schedule. The cancellation had no relationship to this case, but I was saved.

After the shooting, I said good-bye to Doug Bruckner. We had become good friends. He would contact me when I arrived in Lake Tahoe two weeks after the shoot.

On October 3, 1991, Blythe and I finally moved to Lake Tahoe. We were exhausted; I didn't want to see television, cameras, people, anyone. I just wanted to live a normal life, something I hadn't done in years. We were starting over.

Doug called me from Los Angeles to let me know that *Hard Copy* was going to air within the week. I wanted to see how it would turn out; I was excited.

The afternoon of the broadcast, we sat down and watched *Hard Copy*.

"Murder In Paradise"

"Learn how Psychic Dayle Schear took five days to solve a murder: the Diane Suzuki case. Find out why Honolulu police took five years to come to the same conclusion."

Oh, well, so much for promises about police bashing.

Doug called after the television show. "Well, how did you like the story, Dayle? By the way, I tried to soften the story, but my producer decided he would write the ending. Sorry, I had no choice."

I said, "Doug, the story was great. I wish you had gone a little bit easier on the cops. But that's television."

Several weeks passed. I was at my computer writing my book, *Dare to Be Different!* The phone rang—it was Doug.

"Hi, Dayle, I bet you didn't know you were a star."

"What do you mean?" I had no idea what he was talking about.

Doug explained. "Dayle, when *Hard Copy* aired, it also aired in Australia. A lady was watching the show; she was impressed. The lady phoned the television station in Australia. She asked the producer of that show if you could fly to Australia tomorrow morning at eight o'clock to help find her missing daughter. Isn't this exciting! They want me to assist with the story." Doug's voice took on an urgent note. "Dayle, are you listening... are you there...? Can you fly to Australia tomorrow? We can arrange everything. Dayle... are you there...?"

"Yes, Doug, I'm here. I just arrived in Lake Tahoe. I'm not going anywhere, although I'll be glad to work on the case if you want to come to Lake Tahoe." I quickly ended the conversation and continued writing my book, *Dare to Be Different!* I shook my head and smiled as I was typing....

It's funny how life works in mysterious ways. The minute you decide to give it all up, somehow things have a way of turning around and coming back to you. I had a strange feeling I would hear from Doug Bruckner again.

For your enjoyment, I've added the original reports on the Diane Suzuki case from the *Honolulu Star Bulletin* and *Honolulu Advertiser.*

The headlines of the *Honolulu Star Bulletin*, Wednesday November 28, 1990, read as follows:

> ### Police Asks Psychic's Help In Diane Suzuki Case
>
> By Vickie Ong
>
> Psychic Dayle Schear said yesterday that Honolulu police have asked her to take a lie-detector test in connection with the Diane Suzuki case.
>
> Homicide Detective Lt. Gary Dias, however, would not confirm or deny Schear's claim. Suzuki disappeared five years ago

after teaching a class at an Aiea dance studio. Police believe she was murdered.

Schear said Suzuki's family asked her to search the studio two days after the 19-year-old vanished. Schear said she found a pendant belonging to Suzuki, took it home to do a reading on the pendant, then gave it to police.

Schear said police want her to take the lie-detector test to confirm or disprove her claim. Schear said she is scheduled to take the test today. . . .

From Staff and Wire Reports

The *Honolulu Star Bulletin,* November 28, 1990:

Psychic in Suzuki Case Given Lie-Detector Test

By Crystal Kua and David Oshiro

Psychic Dayle Schear says she passed a lie-detector test yesterday in connection with the police investigation into the disappearance and suspected murder of Diane Suzuki.

Police questioning centered on a pendant that Schear said she found in an Aiea dance studio after Suzuki's disappearance in 1985.

The pendant is believed to have belonged to Suzuki, an instructor at the studio who vanished after teaching a class. Police believe she was murdered.

Schear said she became involved with the case at the request of a Suzuki family member a few days after the university student disappeared.

She said she decided to search the studio on a hunch. There she found the pendant, a gold "D" with a diamond, on the floor of the studio in some dust.

At first, she said no one knew if the pendant had actually belonged to Diane. But she asked the family to develop some film and a picture of Suzuki showed her wearing a pendant that looked like the one Schear said she found.

"That's how we knew it was a perfect match," Schear said yesterday while waiting to take her polygraph test.

She took the necklace home to do a "reading" on it and it was then she said she knew that Suzuki was dead. She then gave the pendant to the police.

Police asked her five years ago to take a lie detector test but no one followed up.

"They were angry that I had found something that they hadn't found," Schear said.

After police recently reclassified the Suzuki case a murder, Schear got a call from a Honolulu police detective, again asking her to take the polygraph test.

"What I was able to give today, I think is to prove, without a doubt, that I did not take the pendant and place it there, nor did I make up the story," she said.

"They told me I passed with flying colors," Schear said, adding that police didn't say why they were following up the case now.

"I feel it's all routine. I think they're going along their own lines of whatever they're doing, and they're doing it in order," she said.

Police declined to comment on what Schear said. Schear arrived at the main police station on South Beretania Street with a camera crew. She was shooting scenes throughout the building that may be broadcast on her show, "ESP and You," which runs on Channel 9.

The *Honolulu Advertiser, Wednesday*, November 28, 1990:

Psychic Says She Believes That Diane Suzuki Was Slain

By Vickie Ong, Advertiser Staff Writer

A Psychic who practices what she says is the "art" of seeing into the past, and detectives who rely on police science, have applied their skills in the case of Diane Suzuki, who vanished five years ago.

Honolulu detectives and other experts are continuing their painstaking technical investigation into the circumstantial and physical evidence of the Suzuki case.

Meanwhile, professional Psychic Dayle Schear, who was brought into the case by the Suzuki family, says she is looking into the case through the use of "psychometry, the art of holding on to objects to see into the past, present and future."

Schear, who was hired by the Suzuki family, said she found a pendant at the dance studio within a week of Suzuki's disappearance.

Schear says the pendant with a D on it and a tiny diamond, belonged to Suzuki.

Schear underwent a polygraph examination yesterday to confirm that she found the pendant at the dance studio and did not place it there.

Schear was told by the polygraph examiner she had passed the lie-detector test. Dias said it is against police policy to discuss polygraph results and said he cannot comment on evidence.

Earlier this month, Schear told The Advertiser that after Suzuki's disappearance and while police were conducting their own searches she went to the second-floor dance studio.

She said she was accompanied by a Kailua police lieutenant not assigned to the case, her husband and a 15-year-old friend of Diane's.

Family and friends were unable to confirm that the pendant (which did not have a chain) belonged to Suzuki, Schear said.

But when photographs taken of Suzuki a few weeks earlier were found, she was wearing the same D pendant, Schear said.

She took the pendant home to "do a reading." "It was then that I realized I felt she was telling me that this is where she was and never left there. That's what I believe, and that's where I believe she was murdered," she said.

Police were annoyed that crucial evidence was not turned in immediately. Schear said she submitted the pendant to police in 1985. The police wanted to polygraph her but never did until 1990, five years later.

The *Honolulu Advertiser*, July 13, 1991:

The following article was written about Diane Suzuki's murder, six years after her demise. This article changed my whole life.

Police Search Marsh Close to Suspect's Home

By Vickie Ong, Advertiser Staff Writer

Police investigating the 1985 Diane Suzuki homicide case yesterday dug around in a marsh near the home of a Waiau man who is considered a suspect.

After dozens of officers combed the swampy area from 9 a.m. to 3 p.m. police Homicide Lt. Gary Dias said Suzuki's body was not found, but evidence was recovered.

"No arrests had been made and nothing further will be released at this time," Dias said in a statement.

Since last year, police have said they have a "viable suspect." He was interviewed early in the investigation and his house was searched. The man has never been arrested or charged.

Yesterday's search renewed attention on the six-year-old case of Suzuki, a 19-year-old dance instructor who was last seen about 3 p.m. July 6, 1985, after teaching a class at the Rosalie Woodson Dance Academy in Aiea.

After using special investigative techniques, homicide detectives in November reclassified the missing-person case and declared they believed Suzuki was murdered at the dance studio.

Susan Suzuki, Diane's sister, said police notified her family yesterday morning that they would be "searching a swamp area," but gave no reason that the search was being conducted at this time.

The police work yesterday "just keeps us hopeful, and we've always been hopeful that something (an arrest) will come out of it," Susan Suzuki said last night.

Police homicide detective evidence technicians and members of the Specialized Services Division, including police dogs, were sent to the marsh near a Waiau neighborhood. Waiau is between Pearl City and Pearlridge.

From the road, officers had to make their way 20 feet down a steep embankment choked with California grass and haole koa bushes.

The large marsh is now a dump site for old mattresses, discarded clothing and trash. Police yesterday morning closed off an adjoining street and checked identifications before allowing residents to proceed to their homes.

The search by police came two days after professional Psychic Dayle Schear said on her TV program on the Suzuki case that aired Wednesday, "The body is in water, in a swamp nearby. It's been moved. The clothes have been taken off and put into one place and the body is in another place."

Schear said yesterday that after police declared the case a murder in November, she went to the Waiau home of the suspect "to feel the energy". She said she told police Detective John Isabelo where she felt the body might be.

"I find it so ironic that two days after my show, they go and dig in the spot we've been talking about all along," she said.

Dias told reporters the timing of the search had nothing to do with Schear's program on Wednesday.

Schear, who was brought into the case by the Suzuki family when Diane first disappeared, said last year that she found a "D" pendant, which she believes belonged to Diane, at the dance studio within a week of the woman's disappearance. Schear underwent a polygraph examination about the pendant in November and passed.

Homicide investigators digging in the heavily overgrown Waiau area were working in an area long familiar to them.

On July 20, police with a search warrant went to the Waiau man's house seeking Suzuki's "black leotards, gold necklace chain, gold/pearl earrings, white sneaker-type shoes."

They also received permission to retrieve clothes believed to have been worn by Suzuki's assailant; "shovel or any other implement that may be used for digging"; "developed and undeveloped photographs of Diane Suzuki"; and "the person of Diane Suzuki."

In a police report now sealed by the courts, Detective Isabelo said: "During the search of the home's extension, a plastic trash bag containing detergent-soaked rags was found. One of the shirts in the bag possessed blood-like stains. Laboratory tests indicated that the stain was that of blood."

The police reports and affidavits also disclosed that a Waiau man, now in his 30s, was interviewed twice by police on July 8, 1985, two days after Suzuki disappeared. After the second interview, he underwent a polygraph examination, commonly called a lie-detector test.

The polygraph examiner concluded the suspect was "conclusively deceptive" in his response to questions about whether he knew how Suzuki disappeared or whether he had anything to do with her disappearance.

Detectives also reported they believe a "struggle" had occurred in the bathroom in the Aiea dance studio. Evidence technicians who examined the bathroom in July, 1985 found the wall "appeared to have been cleaned quite thoroughly except for the small pores in the hollow tile."

In November, police returned to the dance studio to use new investigative methods, including laser tests and a chemical called Luminol, which makes blood luminescent even if it's years old and someone has scrubbed away most of it.

Based on these tests, police concluded Suzuki had been murdered.

Update: **On October 22, 1993, the Diane Suzuki case was reopened.**

The city Prosecutor's office issued subpoenas for Grand Jury proceedings, which were closed to the public. Just before Thanksgiving, I was informed that I would be subpoenaed in December, so I planned a trip to Hawaii at that time. I went to Hawaii December 2, but found out the hearing was postponed because they still had two dozen witnesses to examine ahead of me. As of the end of December, I had finished my Hawaii tour and returned to Lake Tahoe.

Meanwhile, KITV Channel 4 in Honolulu got wind of the fact that I was to appear before the grand jury some time in January, and they included the story in their year end recap of the top stories for 1993. In turn, their story was picked up by the Associated Press wire service and distributed nationally.

And the case goes on and on.

CHAPTER 13

HARD COPY AUSTRALIA

October 1991. Blythe and I were settling in nicely after our exhausting move from the islands of Hawaii to Lake Tahoe. After several weeks of unpacking, I settled down to write my book, *Dare to Be Different!* Late in the afternoon my phone rang.

"Hi, this is Dayle. May I help you?"

"Hi, Dayle, this is your long lost friend Doug Bruckner from *Hard Copy.* How ya doing?"

"I'm doing fine. I've been working on my book and everything's coming along nicely."

"Dayle, remember the Australian case I told you about?"

"Yes, vaguely," I said.

"The family of Karmein Chan would like you to help them find their missing daughter in Australia. Can you help?"

"Yes, but I don't want to go to Australia right now. Can the family send her clothing to me in Lake Tahoe?" I asked.

"I'm sure there won't be any problem with that," Doug said.

I specified what I wanted him to do. "Doug, I don't want to know anything about the case. I need you to tell the family to wrap up some of the girl's clothing in individual plastic bags. I need pictures of the girl and a street map of Australia. Please have the family put an "X" on the map where the girl was seen last. Then have the package sent to you at *Hard Copy*. The package must remain unopened until you arrive in Lake Tahoe.

"Please, Doug, under no circumstances do I want you to find out anything about this case. If you learn any information about the girl, I might read your mind. It's better you know nothing," I said.

"Okay, Dayle, sounds good. I'll get back to you within the week."

One week later: "Dayle, I received the package from the Chan family in Australia. We're ready to hire a crew and fly to Lake Tahoe," said Doug. "Can you meet me at Harrah's in the parking lot on Sunday around four o'clock?"

"No problem. Just call me when you arrive and I'll be there," I said.

Blythe and I met Doug at Harrah's that Sunday afternoon. I called in the local press from Reno, and Doug hired his own crew from Sacramento. We were ready to shoot.

The filming started late in the afternoon. The lights and camera were set up in my home. Doug appeared on my doorstep with a package in hand. I greeted him and showed him into the living room. The unopened package was placed on my coffee table while the cameras were rolling.

I sat down nervously and opened the package slowly. I took out the pictures of Karmein Chan and placed them on the coffee table. Next, I pulled out clothing of hers from the box, including her shoes. I touched each object, one by one, until I could focus my attention on the young lady.

The visions were appearing at a very rapid pace. I paused for a moment . . . then I blurted out, *"I'm sorry! She's dead. Karmein was murdered! . . . I see a knife. I don't understand, but I also see a gun. I see a mask. I see a man stalking her and picking her out. I see her in a van. I see sexual molestation. She knows who her killer is. Karmein has seen her killer before. He can't let her go because she recognizes him."*

The cameras kept rolling. I fell to the floor and assumed a position that the body might be found in. I also stated the body would be found within nine months.

After my reading on Karmein Chan, I was handed a piece of paper that lay in the bottom of the box. I had no prior knowledge of this paper or its contents.

The paper read as follows:

From Media Concept to Dayle Schear:
   To give you some background on the case, Karmein Chan, 13 years of age, was abducted from her home in a Melbourne suburb, Templestow, at 9:30 p.m. on Saturday the 13th of April, 1991.

   From the newspaper articles and video you will get a better understanding of the case and the suspect.

   The video also contains some home video taken only days before Karmein disappeared. This vision is the latest photographic material on the girl. The actual photograph was taken some years before when she was in grade four at school.

   As you requested, the package contains personal articles which belonged to Karmein. The video also contains visions of her home and the surrounding area.

   Mrs. Chan contacted us after seeing a story featuring yourself on the Australian version of *Hard Copy*. She has in the past had dealings with a number of clairvoyants, but they've been unable to assist in the case.

We would request most urgently the return of all Karmein's personal effects after you have examined them.

Thank you for your cooperation.

Yours Sincerely,
Richard Willis, Reporter for *Hard Copy*

After a short rest period, Doug turned on the video tape about Karmein Chan. Neither one of us had ever seen the video before.

The film showed Karmein's house in Australia and a car sitting in her circular driveway. Painted on the car were words that no one could make out at first. But the words "Mar to come" were as plain as could be to this Psychic.

I jumped up and shouted, "Doug! Look at that writing on the car. I *can read* the message. It says, *More to come.*"

Doug stopped the tape. He stared at the television screen and said, "You're right; it does look like the words, 'More to come.'"

The television video showed Mrs. Chan in her restaurant in Melbourne. She had left her daughter Karmein, age 13, at home to watch the younger children while she worked.

The next thing we saw was Karmein's mother screaming on television that she wanted her daughter to come home. The tears were streaming down her cheeks.

I turned to Doug. "I know you want me to talk personally to Mrs. Chan; but after seeing the tape, I don't think I can tell her that her daughter is dead."

He said, "I understand, Dayle. Let me think about this for a while. Let's take a lunch break; besides, I need to get out of the house for a while. Mrs. Chan was extremely disturbed about her daughter. I have to think of a way to handle this situation," he said.

Doug and the crew members left for a while. I decided to work on the case to see what else I could come up with. I grabbed one of Karmein's shoes. I closed my eyes tightly and tried to focus. I could see her in a van near her house. This was the first vision that came to mind.

I started to focus on Karmein's killer. Strong impressions came to me. *I knew he was a serial killer. I knew he lived in the red light district of Melbourne. I kept seeing a polar bear; I didn't know what that meant. The killer had black hair and spoke with an accent. He was about 35 years old and about six feet tall. He had scars on his face. He wore leather and had a tattoo on his arm. He worked in a circus at one time. He hung around a school yard and could be hired as a clown for children's parties. One had to be careful; the killer was Psychic.*

I saw the killer as I touched Karmein's picture. He had a knife. I saw rape and molestation. I saw him traveling around with her in the van. She was drugged, then murdered. He disposed of the body no more than fifteen to twenty miles from the Chan family's home.

His motive was very strange. He was angry with the Chan family. I don't know the reason, but the Chans could have done something wrong to this man in the past. I feel he wanted to get even with the family; he wanted to prove a point. I saw that he had frequented the Chan's restaurant on many occasions and had been treated poorly as a customer. He also might have made deliveries to the restaurant at one time.

I was just about to finish with the case when Doug Bruckner came back from his break. "Dayle, did you come up with anything else?"

"Yes, I did." I relayed the new information.

He said, "I'll tell you what. We have to place the phone call to Mrs. Chan soon. Why don't you soften it up a little bit; play it by ear. I'll get the cameras ready. Why don't you relax for a while and formulate your words."

I did just that. We soon placed the call to the Chan family in Australia.

"Hello, Mrs. Chan, this is Dayle Schear, the Psychic," I said.

"Hello, Dayle, I've been waiting for your call."

I paused momentarily. "Mrs. Chan, I'm sorry. I know other Psychics have told you that your daughter is alive, I'm sorry, I don't feel that way." I expected silence on the other end of the phone. This was very hard for me to do; I had to tell the mother that her daughter was dead. I hemmed and hawed about the situation. "Mrs. Chan, are you prepared for what I have to tell you?"

"Yes, Dayle, I am." She replied calmly, but tensely.

"I'm sorry, your daughter is dead. She's been dead from the beginning. I don't know how to tell you how sorry I am." I waited for her reaction.

"I understand, Dayle. I've had nine months to think about this. In my heart I guess I felt she was dead also. Please go on," she begged me.

"Mrs. Chan, I'm sorry . . . Karmein was brutally murdered."

She pleaded, "Tell me what you see, Dayle, please."

"I see a knife. I see a gun. I see a van. I also see sexual molestation. The man entered your house when you weren't home. I see him watching your house. He was casing the place. I see him dressed in some type of uniform. Your daughter let him in; he told her he was sent to the house to fix something. This man knows you and your family. He has eaten at your restaurant. There is something you might have done to this man; he is resentful of your family."

Mrs. Chan interrupted, "I don't know of anyone who is resentful of us. Dayle, you must be wrong."

"I'm not wrong," I said. "Your car was painted with words in the front of your house the day before your daughter was missing. Is that correct? At least that is what I saw on the video tape."

"That's correct. We called the police. They felt it was an unrelated incident," she said.

I quickly disagreed. "I'm sorry, Mrs. Chan, it *wasn't* an unrelated incident. The words on the car spelled out 'More To Come.' Your daughter's kidnapper wrote those words; he wanted to show you how clever he was. Even though you had an alarm system in the house and electronic gates, he was able to get into your home."

I told Mrs. Chan her daughter was buried in dirt. "I can't give you the location. I feel the girl will be found within nine months."

She asked, "If you come to Australia, would you be able to find the body?"

"I don't know; I have to think about it." I replied. "This man is very dangerous. He's Psychic, as well. I think the best I can tell you now is the body will turn up."

Mrs. Chan and I ended the conversation, and Doug ended the taping of the show. He got plenty of footage for *Hard Copy* in Australia and Los Angeles.

Television people are always on the move, ready to forge ahead to their next story. I asked Doug when the story would air, and he said he would call and let me know. Doug also mentioned that I might go to Australia to hunt for the body and the killer. I told him I would think about it.

Shortly after Doug left, I grabbed Karmein's clothing and started to focus once again. This time I could see her killer clearly. *He was letting me watch his every move. I couldn't understand why everything was so vivid. I saw him sitting in his apartment, watching television. I could describe every detail of the apartment. I saw bars on his window and a red light flashing outside the apartment. I saw him wearing jeans.*

I saw him in the van with Karmein. He was wearing a mask; I couldn't see his face. Then something out of the ordinary happened. I heard him speaking to me. "You can watch me kill her," he said.

I jumped back. "Oh, my God, he's talking to me! Blythe, he's talking to me."

"Who's talking to you, Dayle?" Blythe asked.

"The killer. He wants me to watch. He's showing me how he killed Karmein. Oh, my God, he's Psychic! This is a game to him. He wants me to come to Australia."

Blythe remarked, "I don't think so!"

"But Blythe, he won't hurt me. He might show me where she's buried," I said. "But you know what, he'll try to hurt you, Blythe."

I was beginning to scare myself. It was the first time I had felt this way. I was going to track a **Psychic serial killer**. He wanted me to play along with him. I knew I could find him, and I also knew he would lead me to Karmein's body.

The next day I called *Hard Copy* with my findings. They told me they were arranging my trip to Australia.

Several weeks passed. Doug Bruckner called to tell me the segment would air on television in two days.

Two days later we sat down and watched the television show. I must say Doug Bruckner did a wonderful job. The only problem was that the killer now knew what I looked like.

I was warned by several people not to go to Australia, but that didn't stop me. I went ahead and got my visa and waited patiently for *Hard Copy* to call me back.

Several weeks passed; I heard nothing. I expected the family to call, but everything was quiet. I speculated the expenses for me to go to Australia might be overwhelming, considering I might not find the body. Time passed. I never did go to Australia. Maybe I was being protected by the Universe.

Several months later, as I was working in Hawaii, I received a phone call from Doug Bruckner.

"You're not going to believe this," he said. "They found the body of Karmein Chan. You were right; they found her within nine months."

"Where did they find her?" I asked.

"I don't know, but they aired another television show in Australia about your prediction. I should be getting a copy of that soon.

Here's a number you can call in Australia. I think they'll give you all the information you need."

Within moments I was on the phone with *Hard Copy* in Australia. The information relayed to me was written up in an Australian newspaper by Bruce Tobin.

> **Karmein Chan Shot in Panic**
>
> **April 13, 1992:** Police believe the kidnapped schoolgirl Karmein Chan may have been killed after she saw her attacker while being held hostage.
>
> They believe the kidnapper panicked and shot Karmein three times in the head. Detectives believe the skeleton of the young girl found in a shallow grave in an isolated part of Thomastown last Thursday is that of 13-year-old Karmein.
>
> The skeleton was found by a man walking his dogs along Edgars Creek, which runs through an SEC terminal station site, near the corner of Mahoneys Road and High Street. Thomastown is part of an area used for a dumping ground and for land-fill.
>
> Heavy machinery is likely to be brought in to sift through soil where the skeleton was discovered, about 20 minutes from the creek. Police believe the body became exposed after the area had recently been graded and flattened.

Many other articles were faxed to me from Australia after Karmein's body was found.

I found this case to be sad. I knew if I were given a chance, I would have located her killer.

I wish Karmein's mother had been more perceptive. The handwriting on her car that stated "More to come," only one day before Karmein was kidnapped from her home, was a *sign* that her family was in danger.

She might have heeded the warning and made sure her thirteen-year-old child was protected. I found out later that when the kidnapper entered the house, he took Karmein in but hid the two younger children in a closet. They were too little to describe the masked man.

A Psychic Opinion

There seems to be a lesson here to be learned by all parents. Children are our only prized possessions. They should not be left home alone to fend for themselves. No matter how much protection we give them, sometimes it's not enough. In the case of Mrs. Chan, if she or a baby-sitter had been home with the children, maybe this tragedy could have been avoided.

CHAPTER 14

JURY CONVICTS TANDAL

I originally wrote about Roxanne Tandal in my last book, Dare to Be Different! *Since then, more facts have appeared.*

Roxanne Tandal was missing under suspicious circumstances and the police were asking the public's help in finding her. Roxanne had last been seen by her husband when she left for work on a Saturday from her Huehu Street home in Kahuku, Oahu. She never arrived for work as a part-time clerk at Kahuku Full Service Station.

Roxanne's estranged husband told police he had planned to stay in the house with their two sons, 7 and 9, until she returned home. He reported her missing on Monday, police reported.

Kimo Greene, Roxanne's employer, stated, "She was real sweet and considerate, and it's not like her just to walk away like her husband said she did." Greene said he had given Roxanne the day off that Saturday, so she could go to an afternoon baby luau at Haiku Gardens.

Len Ferguson, a friend, escorted Roxanne and the two children to the party. Ferguson said he was told by Roxanne to call her later that evening to confirm plans they had made for the following day. He said he called, but her estranged husband said she wasn't home. That was the last time Ferguson heard from Roxanne Tandal.

"I went to the police Monday about 7:00 p.m. to see if they could check to see if she was okay," Ferguson said. "The police explained that they didn't have the manpower to check up on her. They told me to come back the next day if she was still missing."

Kimo Greene, Roxanne's employer, mounted a search on Thursday throughout the Kahuku area. The search party combed through ten acres of brush, thick vegetation, and rough ridges.

Twenty hours were spent searching the Kahuku area. The family used the help of a Psychic to help find Roxanne; all that they found that day were the skeletal remains of a dog. *Not to confuse the matter, the Tandal family used a different Psychic—not me—at that time.*

Those who knew Roxanne said her disappearance was puzzling, because she was a good mother and would never go anywhere without her two boys. "She'd never leave her kids. She'd do anything for her kids."

Roxanne had recently filed for divorce and was engaged in a bitter custody battle. She fought hard in court for her kids.

The Tandals had separated in April, and a month later a Family Court issued an order to keep Benjamin Tandal away from his wife. The order had expired the month before her disappearance. Friends said she had tried to renew it.

Two weeks after the disappearance of Roxanne, I was called into the case not by the police, but by the family. I had no knowledge whatsoever of this case.

When the Tandal family came to see me, they were frustrated with the response of the Honolulu Police Department. Roxanne had been missing for two weeks, and the police had no clues to her whereabouts. I explained that the Honolulu Police Department did not readily use Psychics in its investigation.

I had asked the Tandals to bring along Roxanne's unwashed clothing, pictures and jewelry. I also asked them to bring a fresh, unopened map of the Honolulu area. Time was of the essence now. If she were alive, we would try to find her. I asked the family to sit down at my dining room table and make themselves comfortable. I slowly placed all the pictures on the table. I always keep a pad and pencil right next to me to record sudden impressions. I held on to a picture of Roxanne in one hand and her jewelry in the other. We opened up a map of the Honolulu area and placed her picture on the map. I let my pencil guide me for information on how to locate Roxanne. This information you are about to read was given to me spiritually.

Transcript of the Tape from the Tandal Case

Roxanne Tandal is not alive. She was murdered. Roxanne knew who her murderer was. There was a brutal fight and argument, leading her to be hit with an object. She was then propped up in a car, made to look like she was still alive, when in fact she had been murdered. Roxanne was wrapped up in a blanket not too far from where she lived. It seems to me I see a shrimp farm nearby. This seems to be a marker of some sort. I see an old air strip nearby, one where planes could land at one time or another. Kahuku Airport, if there is such a place. She is off a dirt road wrapped in a blanket no more than ten feet from this road. If you take all the markers into consideration, you should be able to find the body.

After I channeled this information, I marked the untouched map and gave explicit directions as to where the body would be found and in what position it would be lying. I then described the person with whom she was involved and described her murderer to the family, down to the color of the shirt he was wearing. I found out later how accurate I was. I asked the Tandal family to form a search party to cover the three-mile radius from the shrimp farm to where the Kahuku airport used to be. Her body would lie within this area, off a dirt road, on the left-hand side.

The next day seventy people, family and friends, searched the area I had specified. They found Roxanne Tandal's body exactly where and how I stated it would be. The body was found close to the old Kahuku airport off a dirt road.

I wanted Roxanne's soul to rest in peace. Through my findings on this case, I believe this was a love triangle; jealously was involved. The murder was not done intentionally, but it was done out of anger. However, within six months Roxanne's husband was arrested and charged with her murder.

> **Father Grieves for the Loss of his Daughter**
>
> Roxanne Tandal's father, Ricky Canencia, finally realized that he would never see his daughter alive again. "I don't want to think she's dead," said Canencia, from his Waipahu home.
>
> A father's worst nightmare came true when they found the Tandal body.
>
> "We just want to give her a decent burial now," said Canencia.
>
> Yesterday, Canencia's family consulted a psychic to help decide where to begin looking for Tandal.
> —*The Honolulu Star-Bulletin*

That Psychic was me.

Tandal Convicted of Killing his Wife

A Circuit Court jury yesterday convicted Benjamin Tandal of murdering his estranged wife, Roxanne Tandal, rejecting claims that he was the "wrong man" that was on trial. He claimed he saw her alive the day she disappeared from her Kahuku home last year.

The victim's body was found two weeks later, on New Year's Eve, wrapped in a blanket from her home and dumped in the brush near Marconi Road in Kahuku.

The jury deliberated for seven days, an unusually long time for a criminal case in state court, before returning the verdict. Tandal, 33, did not show any emotion as the verdict was announced, but the victim's father, Ricky Canencia, wept in the gallery. "I love it," Canencia said. "I'm glad, because I know he did it."

Case closed. Tandal is serving time in prison.
—*The Honolulu Star-Bulletin*

About three months later, I had the pleasure of meeting Mr. Canencia. He couldn't thank me enough for helping to find his daughter and putting her soul to rest.

In an article entitled "Psychic Takes Up Residence on the South Shore," that appeared in the *Tahoe Tribune*, on October 27, 1991, Lt. Dias of the Honolulu Police Department did credit me by saying, *"I believe there are gifted people who have the ability to do this. I think for sure that Dayle is one of them."*

People ask me, "Is it all worth it, Dayle?"

My answer is yes, for it's times like this when it makes a difference. If I can help find one missing person, if I can ease the pain of a family and put a soul to rest, then in my heart I know it's all worth while. I know I am doing what God has put me on this earth to do. If I can help but one person in mankind, then I've helped a generation to see the light that shines from above.

CHAPTER 15

PETER HURKOS

Peter Hurkos technically died on June 1, 1988. His death left numerous people in disarray, including his wife Stephany and daughter Gloria. He was loved by many, including myself.

Peter was born May 21, 1911, in Holland. Peter was considered to be the foremost Psychic of the century.

When I was about twelve years old, I used to watch Peter on television using psychometry, the art of holding on to objects to see into the past, present, or future. I was fascinated beyond belief. Peter was amazing. Little did I know the universe had picked me to become his successor. This must have been a tall order for the universe, for who could fit into this man's enormous shoes? Surely not I.

My own Psychic ability began to emerge professionally when I was about twenty-seven, and at the age of thirty-two our paths crossed.

I was introduced to Peter by Doug Bushousen, head of entertainment for Harrah's in Lake Tahoe. Before Peter would accept me as his student, I had to pass several tests, which were given to me by his wife, Stephany. Our friendship and training spanned well over six years.

Peter specialized in Psychic detective work for families and government. He wanted me to follow in his footsteps. I was curious; I always wanted to know more about ESP. I would listen, watch and learn. The time spent with this man was never enough; I could have studied with Peter for at least twenty years or more. After extensive training, Peter felt I was ready to work beside him.

However, on many occasions I became frustrated with the testing Peter and Stephany administered to me, especially when Peter was teaching me how to bend a spoon or a fork without touching it.

I watched him intently concentrate on a metal spoon. The perspiration ran down his forehead. Without touching the spoon, Peter would bend and twist it in many directions right before my eyes. Amazing! Peter would glance at me and say, "Now it's your turn, Dolly. Just concentrate: that's all you have to do. It's mind over matter. You can do it."

I was intimidated. I kept wondering how a spoon could bend backwards without someone touching it. It was mind boggling. It must be a trick, I told myself. No, Peter detested trickery of any kind. Then why wasn't my spoon bending? I glanced at Peter, eyes cast downward; I was ashamed.

As Peter walked away confidently, he shouted, "Dolly! You don't believe! That's why your spoon won't bend."

He wanted me to believe that my mind could bend the spoon. I tried, but my rational mind always took over. Through the years, I've picked up a spoon now and then; most of the time my spoon would bend about a quarter of an inch. No match for my master.

I've always had a rational mind. I knew I had a gift, something very precious, and through this gift I have been able to help people transform their everyday lives. One of my main goals in life was to maintain my normality. Might I mention, this was quite a task;

there were times that I questioned my sanity, especially when Peter was alive.

Peter and I would have long discussions regarding spirits and afterlife. Unlike Peter, who believed in everything, it was very hard for me to believe in spirits and things-that-go-bump-in-the-night. It wasn't until Peter's passing that my whole thinking about life changed.

I learned of Peter's death while I was working in Hawaii. I explained to Stephany by phone my aversion to attending funerals. My own belief system allowed me one private thought, that when one dies, the soul is no longer in the body or remotely at the grave.

However, the events that were to take place within the next forty-eight hours would bewilder my mind and change my thinking about the spirit world forever.

It all started in the afternoon. Stephany wanted me to attend temple to say a prayer for Peter. After temple, Stephany reached into her car for a tape recorder. She asked me to run into a local drug store and purchase a sixty-minute, unopened cassette tape. I did.

When I handed her the tape, I asked, "What's this for?"

Steph remarked, "Never mind, I was told to do this after Peter died." She also reminded me that Peter had told her long before his passing that I wouldn't be at his funeral anyway. However, he added that if I didn't show up at their home within six months to pay my respects, Steph should disown me. Thank God I made it on time.

Peter had given Steph instructions to place the tape recorder at his grave and walk away. So we did. The premise was he would try to communicate to us from the grave. Whoa! This was mind boggling.

"You mean a dead person can talk? How can that be?" I thought. "Oh, well, if anyone can do it, Peter can. Why, he can do anything." After the tape recorder was placed alongside the grave, we went for a bite to eat. After an hour or so, we drove back to the grave site and retrieved the tape recorder.

Upon arriving home, Steph carefully turned the tape recorder on. There were several people gathered at her home for this event. We sat around the table, listening intently.

As the tape was playing, I heard on it a series of strange things. There was silence at first, then the sound of a gust of wind, although when we had gone to the grave site that day, it was as calm as could be. The wind grew louder and louder on the tape. Within moments, there was a faint voice on the tape; I could barely make it out. I pinned my ear to the tape recorder as I turned the volume up.

I heard a male voice shouting, " Stephany! Stephany! Get the doctor." I recognized the voice. It was Peter. I turned the volume up higher and higher so everyone in the room could hear. Over and over again Peter was shouting, "Stephany, get the doctor. Help me! I'm falling; get the doctor!"

His voice was so real that I turned to Steph and said, "Stephany, help Peter. He wants a doctor." I had to snap back to reality when I realized it was only a tape recorder and Peter was dead. On the tape I could hear children laughing and playing in the background. Yet this was an adult grave site; there were no children present. The children were definitely from beyond. I realized after the tape was over that Peter was telling me how he died. I asked Steph for the rest of the details about Peter's death.

"It's on the tape, Dayle. The day Peter died we were leaving the doctor's office. The doctor gave him a clean bill of health. As Peter and I were walking down the stairs, he knew something was wrong; he was angry with the doctor for not seeing the problem. When we got to the bottom of the stairs and started to walk to the car, Peter collapsed. He held my hand tightly and shouted, 'Steph, get the doctor! Get the doctor!' Don't you see, Peter wanted you to know how he died."

Everyone present heard the tape that day.

What more can I say? This skeptic-now-turned-believer knows without a doubt that the spirit lives on. I knew there was no way for anyone to have put Peter's voice on that tape.

My next spiritual adventure started on the first anniversary of Peter's death. The first anniversary of a person's death is supposed to be sacred. The spirit comes back to greet all of that person's friends on that day. Blythe and I were in Los Angeles to pay our respects.

That evening Stephany and Gloria, Blythe and I and Paul, Peter's life-long friend, went to temple to pay our respects. The service for Peter was going along very nicely, when Stephany grabbed my hand tightly.

"Peter is here. Can you feel him? He's grabbing my hand!" she shouted. "There he is! Can you see him?"

"Steph, I can't see him. Where is he?"

"Dayle, he's right next to me; I can feel him. Oh, my hand! It's hurting; he's holding my hand too tightly."

Stephany's voice grew louder. I turned to Blythe; he was staring at Stephany. She was standing in an awkward position, leaning on someone. But no one was there. We decided the stress was too much for her. It was time to take Stephany home.

When we arrived at Peter's home, Stephany made herself comfortable. We sat around the table, talking to each other about Peter and how amazing he was. Without warning, Paul began moaning and groaning. He was disturbing our conversation.

Within moments, Paul became the persona of Peter Hurkos. He spoke in Peter's language, which was Dutch. Then he switched back to English. Our mouths hung open. Paul doesn't speak Dutch. Nor is he a channeler or a medium. We sat in bewilderment. Peter's voice was coming out of Paul's mouth.

Paul's eyes had the same piercing look that Peter's once had. Paul slowly turned to Blythe and gave him a reading. He said, "Someone is stealing you blind. You must watch out. You will lose $18,000. They are stealing you blind." Paul went on to name the person who was taking money from Blythe.

"I want you to take care of Stephany," he said, "and watch over Gloria." We were hanging on to every word. Then Paul snapped out of it; he began talking in his normal tone of voice, just as if nothing had ever happened.

"Paul, do you realize what happened?" I asked.

"No," he answered. "Why?"

"Peter was able to use your body to speak. He gave Blythe a reading through you," I said.

"Dayle, you're crazy!" Paul remarked. "Peter didn't come through me. Come on!"

But Stephany had managed to tape some of the reading. We let Paul listen as he shook his head in disbelief. "I think it's time for me to go. I have to digest everything that happened tonight. See you folks later."

Blythe and I decided to retire as well; it was late, and Stephany was fading. We didn't want to discuss what happened. It was all too bewildering.

Blythe and I went to our room. "Do you think Paul was faking it?" I asked.

"I don't think so."

"But we don't have $18,000. What does he mean?"

"I don't know, Dayle, but we'll find out."

Months later, in Hawaii, we found out what Peter was trying to forewarn us about.

Blythe made his living by producing Psychic fairs on Oahu. He was very successful at producing the fairs, until we noticed someone beginning to copy his fairs. Our nest egg was dwindling slowly. The more the fair was copied, the less money there was. It was becoming impossible to produce a Psychic fair; we now were losing money. Peter was right. To top it all off, the person named at Stephany's house was the very person who was copying Blythe's Psychic fairs. And the amount of the loss, $18,000, was accurate as well, over a period of time.

Then we realized that Peter's spirit was alive. He could speak through other people. Peter would warn us whenever trouble was near. Not only did he come through Paul, but he also came through many Psychic friends of ours. My Psychic friends became human telephones for us. I received warnings from Peter on many occasions

On one particular occasion, I placed a phone call to Paul. During the conversation, he faded out and Peter came in. Through Paul, Peter warned me of a bomb. I was to be careful; he saw something exploding around me. Peter said it had the letter "S" on it. He wanted me to stay out of parking areas. "I want you to be careful!" he shouted.

A month passed. Blythe and I were in Hilo on an Outer Island tour. That day we turned on the television and watched the San

Francisco earthquake live. We saw buildings falling, underpasses totaled, parking areas demolished. Peter had been trying to warn me of the San Francisco earthquake.

I seemed to be having an on-going conversation with Peter. But whom could I talk to about this? Everyone I knew would think I had lost it. So Blythe and I kept a journal. We logged my conversations with Peter and tested the accuracy each and every time. We asked for confirmation from the spirits, to ensure it was Peter who was coming through. The accuracy was incredible. Every Psychic friend I had was beginning to have Peter encounters. We decided to research this matter a little further. I wanted to know why this was happening. I placed a call to Stephany and explained the Peter episodes. I wanted to know what they meant.

Stephany explained that when a person dies, the spirit lives on. If the spirit can find a person willing to let it use his or her body, it will try to come through and communicate messages from the other side. Stephany felt Peter wanted to channel information through me. I told her that I didn't want my body to be used as a channel. Stephany responded, "There's your answer. Since you won't allow Peter to come through you, he has to use other people to communicate messages to you."

Now I had the answer, although this was very hard for me to accept at first. But as the years passed, I learned to accept whatever Peter told me. The only condition I set up between myself and other Psychics was that there had to be proof beyond a reasonable doubt that the information they were giving me was coming from Peter Hurkos. There is an old adage from the Bible: test your spirits wisely; be sure they come from God. I set the rules. Peter has always come through.

Several years after Peter's death, I contacted Paul, Peter's friend, on a whim. Once again Paul faded out and Peter came in with a full-on reading. This time I was totally unprepared for what he was about to tell me.

Peter told me he was concerned about a leak I was having in my house. Several weeks later, the leak occurred in the very spot he was referring to.

He also told me of a life-threatening situation. He wanted me to call Blythe into the room. I did. Then Peter told me to ask Blythe why the soles of his sneakers were broken. I repeated to Blythe what Peter had said. Blythe looked bewildered. "How did he know I had worn my sneakers to the sole and the flaps were exposed?"

"I don't know, Blythe. I'm on the phone talking to Paul, and Paul has turned into Peter. Now Peter is asking about your sneakers. I didn't know anything about your sneakers. This is blowing my mind. Paul is not Psychic in any way, shape or form. And besides, how would he know about your sneakers? This is getting heavy."

Peter went on. "Tell Blythe to throw away those sneakers immediately, or he is going to fall and break his neck." Blythe threw the sneakers out.

Then Peter went on to describe my car, which was parked in front of my house. Not only did he describe the color, but he also told me I should be aware of a nail in one of the tires. How did he know I always kept one car outside the house because my garage is too small? No one but my neighbors knows that one. Several weeks later, a nail was found in my left front tire, exactly as he had described it.

Peter then said something so amazing that even today it blows my mind. He was worried about my left back tooth. He wanted me to go to the dentist; he said my tooth was exposed. I assured him that my tooth was fine; I had just been to the dentist earlier that afternoon. Peter insisted something was wrong. Two days later, while I as talking on the phone, the crown of my tooth loosened and popped out, exposing my left back molar. I ran to the dentist with crown in hand. What more can I say? I've ruled out telepathy. And, in my heart, I know Peter is guiding me.

After his passing and throughout the years, Peter has been by my side. My latest adventure was in Hawaii. A young lady named B.J. came to me for a reading. After the reading was over, B.J. mentioned she had been in contact with my teacher, Peter Hurkos, and he had a message for me.

Here we go again, I thought.

I asked what the message was. B.J. stated that Peter had told her I was going to move to the mainland. I was going to write a book for the world to see. My time was up in Hawaii, and I had to move on. My move would take place in a few months, before the new year would end.

I looked at her dumbfounded. "B.J., I've been thinking of moving back to the mainland to write my book. You must be reading my mind."

"No! Peter told me."

"But how will this happen?" I responded.

"There will be a lady who will buy your house. You will be taken care of throughout the time of your writings. Fame will come to you on the mainland. You must carry on with Peter's work. I promise you, this will happen. Call me when it does."

Well, several weeks after the prediction was made, I decided to move to Lake Tahoe. I contacted my dear friend Marion and asked if she wanted to buy my house. Marion helped me out, and I was able to purchase the home of my dreams in Lake Tahoe. To hear the story in detail, read my first book, *Dare to Be Different!* The story I've just told you is not as simple as I've written it here.

Peter told me the move to the mainland was to occur, but I still had to guide the people of Hawaii. I still would have shows and perform in the islands. B.J. was right. I called her. "Thanks once again, B.J., for letting yourself be used as a human telephone."

Once again there was proof that Peter's spirit is alive. Most of the conversations I've had with Peter have been taped and put away in a safe place, just to ensure my sanity, if nothing else.

Peter, I miss you with all my heart. I wish you could be here in the flesh. But for now, in spirit will do. I love you, Peter, and I know wherever you are in the great heavens, you will always be there for me and for your family.

You helped save so many souls when you were alive, and now you're saving souls from beyond. Peter, it's nice to know we just don't die and that our spirit lives on. You've more than proven this to me. God bless you, and keep up the good work. I'll be waiting to hear from you soon.

Love,
Dayle and Blythe and family.

CHAPTER 16

LISTEN! TO THE UNIVERSE

Blythe and I had planned our Hawaii trip since early in July.

Checking with every Psychic I knew, I was told that my book, *Dare to Be Different!*, was going to be a success. However, the Psychics also predicted there would be a delay involving my book. I never understood why. Delay! Delay! Delay! The Psychics predicted a delay. What could possibly delay this book? The presses were rolling. Everything was going smoothly. They must be wrong, I thought.

Now that I look back on the spiritual and sequential events that led to our Hawaii trip, if I knew then what I know now, I would have planned matters differently. Or would I?

It all started in April of 1992. We were in the Islands, working and looking for a distributor for *Dare to Be Different!* This was the only way we could get it accepted by Walden Book Store. Lucky for us, there were two distributors on Oahu, Pacific Trade Group and Book and Video. I called one of the local bookstores to see which one it would recommend. I was told that Pacific Trade Group was under reorganization. I decided to go with Book and Video.

The Universe had provided me with someone I knew. The owner of Book and Video was Joe Sovan, someone I was familiar with. In the past, Joe had mass produced my tarot video, *Tarot for Beginners.*

That April, I consulted with several prominent businessmen in the Islands about what they thought of the distributor I had chosen. They told me Joe was in trouble financially. "Be very careful; this man could go under," they warned me.

Did I listen? No, of course not! I was in a hurry to get a distributor for my book. Since Joe was the only game in town, I needed him, I told myself.

When Blythe and I entered Joe's office, I noticed Blythe was ill at ease with the man. This was unusual; Blythe likes nearly everyone.

I confronted Joe about his business. "Joe, I heard your business is in trouble and you may be going bankrupt." I said.

Joe responded, "Dayle, my video business is going bankrupt; however, my book business is very stable. In fact, I expect the book business to pull me out of the hole. Don't worry. My company is very sound."

I explained to Joe how important my book was to me. "We put everything into this book—$30,000 in a second mortgage—and I gave up most of my house to write *Dare to Be Different!* We want you to know there can't be any screw-ups. Do you understand?"

Joe nodded and handed me a contract.

We left the office. Blythe did not trust Joe. As for me, I didn't listen to anyone; I just kept steam-rolling ahead. We returned to Lake Tahoe in early May with contract in hand. It would be several months before we'd sign with Joe.

In July, I received a phone call from Dick Grimm of KGMB-TV in Hawaii. Although I didn't realize it then, this was the first of many warning signs to come.

"Hi, Dayle, when are you planning your next television show?" he asked.

I replied, "Well, the book will be ready in September. I'd like to go live in October."

Dick immediately stopped me. "No, Dayle, you can't; it's election time. There won't be any available spaces. I can't preempt television programing, due to the election."

I was confused. "Dick, my book is coming out. You're asking me to sit on 10,000 copies until spring. If I do that, I'll be bankrupt!" I screamed. "You know I put my heart and soul into this book. What am I going to do?"

"Now calm down. I'll call you back in a few hours. We'll think of something," he said.

I relayed the conversation to Blythe. "That's it," he reminded me. That's the delay all the Psychics are talking about—the election."

I wasn't convinced. "We knew about the election in May. Everyone told us we had nothing to worry about. Now we have something to worry about."

"Just sit tight and wait for Dick to call us back," he said.

Several hours later, Dick called. "Dayle, the only spot I can give you is late night on a Saturday. Why don't you think about it and call me back."

After I hung up the phone, I looked at Blythe as though my whole world had caved in. "What are we going to do? Late night on Saturday? The election. What next? Why is this happening to me? Maybe we should cancel the whole thing and wait till spring. I know! We can promote in Washington or Oregon or Nevada."

Blythe shook his head. "Dayle, the election is everywhere. It doesn't matter where we promote; we'll have the same problem anywhere we go. You have two choices: either take the late night in Hawaii or wait until spring," he said.

I sighed. "I guess we'll go to Hawaii. We'll postpone the Outer Island tour and concentrate all our efforts in Honolulu."

I called Dick. "We'll take the late night show in October," I said, rather dazed. Dick informed me the show would air at 11:00 p.m. He was sorry. Great, the whole state is sleeping by 10:00 p.m., I thought. But I decided to make the most of it.

The next day we scheduled all our autograph sessions. We started with Liberty House, which was including me in it's November 8th promotion, the biggest one they had ever held. Then there was Walden Books; we were to appear at each and every Walden bookstore on Oahu. Next we scheduled guest appearances at Honolulu Book Stores throughout the Island. Oh, well, things weren't turning out so badly. With all these promotions in Honolulu, I knew I would sell a lot of books. I decided to promote in December as well; starting in March of 1993, we would go live on the air and then do my outer island tour. Things would work out.

We worked diligently on my book as the months passed. Early in September, Blythe and I heard there was a hurricane heading for the Islands. Blythe looked at me. "Well, what do you think?"

"I think the hurricane is going to hit. I feel it," I said. "Besides, Hawaii is overdue. I remember the last hurricane, hurricane Iwa. I was there. I hope I'm wrong."

Days passed; we watched the television news intently. It was September 11, 1992. Hurricane Iniki was heading dead on for the Hawaiian Islands. The winds were clocked at over 150 miles an hour. Oh, my God! What next? *Another sign!* The hurricane was going to hit Honolulu! We watched television relentlessly. Within hours, Hurricane Iniki made a radical turn and hit the island of Kauai. Total devastation.

Honolulu was hit, but not as hard. There were certain areas that looked as though they had been bombed; but, all in all, everything was fine. Kauai, on the other hand, was devastated. And so were her people. Thousands of people lost their means of living.

After the hurricane I began to wonder. I wasn't so sure I was supposed to go to the Islands. I felt for the people of Kauai. I didn't think this was the proper time to be promoting my book. I wanted to help, but I didn't know how.

A month later, it seemed life was getting back to normal, in Honolulu at least. People were going about their business as usual. I asked a few people at KGMB if I should attempt to promote my book in the Islands. The answer was yes. So, against all odds we decided to continue.

September 29, Blythe and I were about ready for our trip to Hawaii. As I did some last minute shopping around town, I heard on the car radio that Highway 50 and Echo Summit were closed due to a fire raging out of control. The fire was in the Kyburz area, thirty miles from our home. I raced up the hill toward home. I was freaking out. Another *sign!* Now I knew I was not supposed to go to Hawaii.

"Blythe," I screamed, "they closed Highway 50! They closed our main road. How are we supposed to get to San Francisco?"

"Calm down. Don't worry. I doubt if the road will remain closed. The tourists have to come up somehow," he said.

We were riveted to the television as the fire raged on, worsening by the minute.

Helen, our house sitter, was watching my dogs. I asked her opinion. "Should I go to San Francisco, or should I just give it all up?"

Helen said, "Dayle, go. Don't worry. You'll make it to the Bay Area."

I told her, "I'll sleep on it tonight. If I feel it's okay in the morning, we'll go."

The next morning there was only a ten percent containment of the fire. It was still headed in our direction. But I felt we should go to Hawaii, because we had promised to be there. My television show was still on for October 3, and at least I could do my readings, if all else failed.

So off we went. We had to drive all the way around the lake just to reach Highway 80, an alternate route to San Francisco. It took us over two hours to reach the Truckee area, heading for the Bay Area. We got word that the highway patrol might be closing Highway 80. That was all that we needed. If that had occurred, I would have canceled everything. As luck would have it, we made it into the Bay Area in time.

We stopped at my attorney's house in Mill Valley. That's where Blythe and I always leave our car for the duration of our stay in the Islands. I recall checking my watch; our plane was leaving the Bay Area at 2:30. "Well, let's get ready to go to the airport," I shouted.

"Wait," Blythe said. "Call United and check on our flight to see if it's on time."

"Why?" I responded. "This plane is always on time."

"Just call!" he said.

I complied and called United to check on Flight 818 to Honolulu.

"Just a moment," said the lady on the line. There was a long pause. Then, "Sorry, Ms. Schear, your plane has been delayed by six hours." Another sign!

I couldn't believe what I was hearing. "What? You're joking! You must be joking!" I squirmed and shouted the bad news to Blythe across the room. I told the reservations clerk I would take a plane the next morning instead of waiting six hours.

"Blythe, this is another sign that we are not meant to go to Hawaii," I said dejectedly.

He replied, "Well, it's too late now. KGMB has been promoting us. We have to go to Hawaii. Let's just make the best out of this situation."

The next morning everything seemed to be fine. I called home and the fire was turning away from our area, but the main road into Lake Tahoe still remained closed.

Bright and early, we boarded the plane and headed for Honolulu. When we arrived in Hawaii, it was October 1st. We were safe and sound. Little did we know what lay ahead of us.

We finally got settled in, and our television show aired at eleven o'clock Saturday evening. The next morning we picked up our phone calls. Just as I suspected, the viewership was down tremendously due to the time slot. My readings were trickling in.

Within a few hours, people were calling and telling us that my book was unavailable on the outer islands. Blythe and I looked at each other. We didn't understand. We had let Joe Sovan know about our promotion and he had promised us that all bookstores would be stocked. We tried endlessly to reach Joe that weekend; his secretary informed us he was unavailable. I started to panic; I knew something was wrong.

Early Monday morning I heard from Joe. I was agitated. "Where have you been? We have been trying to get ahold of you."

Joe replied, "Dayle, I'm sorry, but . . . but . . . you'd better pick up the rest of your books at my warehouse. I'm declaring bankruptcy."

My mouth dropped. I was shocked! "Blythe," I screeched, "Joe is declaring bankruptcy!"

Not only did Joe declare bankruptcy, but he also sold 500 of my books and collected most of the money for himself. He claimed he had tried everything but just couldn't make it. Poor Joe?

I lay my head down on my desk. It was the first time in years that tears came to my eyes. My book, *Dare to Be Different!*, was my baby, and my baby was dying. I just stared at Blythe. He was somewhat in shock, but not surprised. He hadn't trusted Joe from the beginning.

What upset me the most was that I had to go through this experience, no matter what. I didn't have a choice. It didn't matter which distributor I used; the outcome would have been the same. I could have chanced it with Pacific Trade Group, but they were on the verge of reorganizing. Maybe I wouldn't have lost 500 books, but I would have had an ulcer. I don't know which was worse. Well! All the signs were there; the Universe was trying to warn me all along. Why didn't I listen?

This one event triggered everything else that went wrong. I sat around my house for several days, trying to figure a way out of this mess. Not only had I put my heart and soul into *Dare To Be Different!*, but I had also pulled a second mortgage and taken a year off from work just to write my book. And, I broke a cardinal rule: never put all your eggs in one basket.

I know that 500 books doesn't sound like much, but in round figures I lost about $7,000 in sales right off the bat. To top it all, I made nothing off whatever books were left in the stores. I never could understand this, but there was a rule that all monies from sales had to go to Joe Sovan, no matter what—until I found another distributor. Since my book was a new release, there were about 200 copies left on the shelf. I started scrambling.

Within two days I found myself a new distributor, called Bookline. Bookline used to be Pacific Trade Group. The company had called back its original owner, reorganized and gained strength, and was growing. I guess I was meant to be with them all along. I now had a new distributor. I just had to wait for the 200 books to sell before I would see a dime.

My next move was to cancel most of my autograph sessions. I felt defeated. All monies would go to Joe Sovan, anyway, so why bother. I worked in the Islands for thirty days nonstop, trying to recoup some of my money. I still had to pay for the television show and newspaper ads promoting my book. This set me back about $15,000. I was virtually working for nothing. I couldn't see the light at the end of the tunnel.

I was lucky, though, in a way, for before my book first came out, I presold several copies, and from the letters I received, I knew my book was a hit, a success. At least I knew I could write. You know that old saying "I'm great, but know one knows it." Well, that's me. I can't explain how it feels when you take the ball to the finish line, and there's no one there to greet you.

Why didn't I listen? Hard head! I had thought I was invincible.

Time to Listen to the Universe:

1. When KGMB's Dick Grimm changed the time of my television show, that was a major sign. I should have heeded the warning. I knew the eleven o'clock hour was out of my reach. I knew that half the population in Hawaii would be sleeping; therefore, no one would know I had a book out.

2. The election. Who can compete with a presidential election?

3. Joe Sovan. We were clearly warned about him in the beginning. However, I felt sorry for him and wanted to give him a chance.

4. Hurricane Iniki. Now, who can compete with a hurricane?

5. The fire in Lake Tahoe. All the roads were closed for a reason. Next time a road closes, I'll just stay put. I've learned my lesson.

6. The delay of my plane was a clear warning to turn around and go back home.

The grand finale was Liberty House. This was to be my chance to recoup some of my money. I couldn't wait for its promotion. Since Liberty House was my own account, the money from every book sold would go to me. But Liberty House had other plans. I received a phone call from one of the department heads.

Liberty House had decided to delay its big promotion on November 8, due to a concert scheduled that same day to benefit the victims of Hurricane Iniki on Kauai. The autograph session would be changed from the 8th to the 21st. Would I still be in the Islands?

That was it for me! "No!" was my response. It was time to go home. I finally got the message.

Before leaving the Islands, I checked with several Psychics and numerologists to find out what had gone wrong, something I should have done in the beginning.

Next lesson: always check your numerology chart before starting a new venture. I found out I was a number nine; I was in my ninth year, a year of karma. I was winding up all my old problems. The following year, 1993, would be better for me, the beginning of a new cycle. I was told to go home and stay put; anything else I started in 1992 would be a total failure. Go home and wait till

March of 1993, was the message. And you know what? I believed it.

Blythe and I caught the next plane home. Lake Tahoe was a breath of fresh air.

Hereafter, I plan to listen to the Universe. I learned that when things go wrong, stay put; don't open the door. Wait till the debris clears. Always trust your instincts and, above all, listen to the Universe.

CHAPTER 17

EVERY PSYCHIC NEEDS A PSYCHIC

As far back as I can remember, fortune tellers and Psychics have always fascinated me. My first encounter with a fortune teller was unique.

I was only twelve years old when the Ringling Brothers/Barnum and Bailey Circus came to town. I watched as they carefully put up the tents. I gathered some wooden boxes to stand on and stared with excitement and awe through a metal fence at the clowns prancing around. I saw the tallest man and the shortest man in the world and a huge fat lady and a man with tattoos all over his body.

I thought to myself, how wonderful it must be to be a part of the circus. You can travel and see the world. How exciting my life would be if only I could join the circus.

I made my decision right then and there, and I ran home to pack my things. When my mother walked into my room, she asked in amazement, "Dayle, why are you packing your clothes at seven o'clock in the evening? Where are you going?"

I stuttered and said, "I'm going to visit my girlfriend Adrienne down the street." This seemed to appease my mother.

I went through all the coats and jackets in the house to see how much money I could muster. Luck was on my side; I found a five-dollar bill. That was a lot of money in those days. I left my house in a wispy cloud of dust and jumped aboard my trusted bicycle, with a knapsack of clothes on my back. I was off to join the circus.

It was nightfall; the circus was all lit up. Music was playing and the barkers were barking. In the distance I could hear, "Come here, kid; knock down all the milk bottles and win a prize." My eyes grew bigger. I couldn't believe all the fascinating sounds and sights that were surrounding me. I had popcorn in one hand and cotton candy in the other. Soon my money would all be gone.

Then, out of the corner of my eye, I spotted a sign that read *Gypsy Fortune Teller.* A short, old, fat lady came out from her tent. She asked me if I wanted my palm read. "Can I read your future, young lady?"

No one had to tell me what that meant; even though I was 12, I somehow knew. My memory was jarred back to a time when my parents and I were driving along a road I was not familiar with. The area was called Gypsy Town. My mother turned to me abruptly. "Dayle," she said, "close your eyes. Don't look. This is where the gypsies live. If you're not careful, they will put a curse on you."

I asked what a gypsy did. And mom said, "They read your future, then they take your money. They have power, you know."

Dad yelled, "Don't scare the kid!"

Mother was frightened and superstitious, I thought.

Now, here I was at the circus and the gypsy wanted to read my palm. I was scared. "Come here, come closer," she said. My knees were shaking. I handed her the last of my money and held out my palm.

"Young lady, I see you have much money in your lifetime." She bent my hand downward. "I see you're going to be famous. Ah, but you've run away from your family." How did she know that? "Your family, they miss you. They wonder where you are."

I looked up and said, "I want to join the circus; that's why I ran away."

Tears were pouring down my little cheeks.

"I think it's time for you to go home, before something terrible happens," she warned.

I pulled my hand away and went racing home to my mother. I thought the gypsy was going to curse me.

I never told my mother where I went. But I'll always remember the gypsy who read my future.

Throughout the years that followed, I was always fascinated by the future. As years passed, I became a professional Psychic. I chose this profession because I always wanted to help people. Money was secondary.

I noticed it was hard to read for myself; the pictures weren't always clear. Yet, when I read for someone else, I was right on the money.

Whenever, I had the chance, I would sneak away for a reading now and then, just to see how accurate everyone else was. More times than not, I was disappointed with the readings I received from various Psychics; very few were accurate.

However, while living in L.A., I came across what I consider to be great Psychics. One who comes to mind was an old lady in her seventies who lived in our building. I visited her on many occasions. I knew she was Psychic. "It takes one to know one," the saying goes. She would take out her cards whenever I came to visit. The cards were called the *Gong Hee Fot Choy* method of reading. She would carefully lay out the cards and study them endlessly.

One day she looked up at me and said, "You know, Dayle, you're going to be famous."

I smiled and asked her to go on.

"I see a robbery. It looks like your car is being robbed," she stated. "I want you to be very careful of this. I also see you're going to move, change apartments, in the near future. Check with me in the near future."

I thanked her and left.

The next day I went to check on my car; sure enough, the elderly lady was right. The top from my Bug Eye Sprite convertible was missing; someone had stolen it. And, within a month I was accepted as the new apartment manager of our building, which brought about a change in apartments. She was right again. As far as my fame was concerned, it would be years later before this would occur.

Then there was the great Dr. Richard Ireland. I first met Richard while he was appearing at a local nightclub in Honolulu. Richard's act was special; till this day I've never seen anything like it.

He was a billet reader, one who reads serial numbers off an unseen dollar bill. Richard could read those numbers a mile away. It always amazed me. He would also appear on stage blindfolded and answer questions from the audience.

Richard predicted my future on many occasions and was about ninety-five percent accurate. At one point in my life he asked me if I wanted to train with him. I turned him down because by then I was working with Peter Hurkos.

Then there was Dr. Don Torres, one of the most amazing Psychics I've ever encountered. He saw fifteen years into my future, with an accuracy rating of ninety-five percent. Amazing!

Don told me of my nephew's death. He told me I would be living in one state and working in another; I would have two marriages; I would become a nationally renowned Psychic; I would write a series of books. He went on and on. Some of the things Don told me are still coming true.

Then there was my teacher, Peter Hurkos. Besides teaching me to finesse my ability, Peter read me on a daily basis. His accuracy rate into the future was 99%. He rarely missed.

It was through Peter that I met another wonderful Psychic, Mel Doerr. Peter told me how talented Mel was, and through the years we've become the best of friends.

I decided, while writing this book, to interview several of the Psychics who I feel are very talented. Over the years I've searched the world to find talented Psychics; I've found only a handful.

Mel Doerr is one of them. He was born in Louisville, Kentucky, on March 22, 1954. Mel is a renowned professional Psychic, specializing in psychometry, the art of holding on to objects to see into the past, present, or future.

Mel works in the Chicago area and is a regular on many radio talk shows. He has performed on *Life-Style*, a local cable television show, and on *North-Show-Tonight*, a Fox 32 program.

Mel's ability is genetic, passed on through many generations by the male side of the family. His grandfather was extremely psychic.

Mel's earliest memory of his ability was of the day his grandfather died. Mel was only six. When his mother picked him up from school, he blurted out, "Grandpa died!" His mother was astonished. How did he know that?

Mel's ability scared his mother, so she cautioned him not to say frightening things. Mel hid his talent for many years; he didn't want anyone to think he was strange.

Peter wanted me to test Mel's ability and suggested I call Mel. When I heard Mel say hello over the phone, I exclaimed, "Oh my god, you are Psychic!"

"Who is this?" Mel asked.

"Sorry to bother you, Mel; this is Dayle Schear. I'm training with Peter Hurkos and he wanted me to call you. Peter tells me you're very talented."

"Sorry, Dayle. You caught me in the bathtub. Can I call you back? I'm dripping wet," he said.

"No problem," I answered.

That's how we met in 1982, and we've been friends ever since.

I asked Mel about some of the outstanding cases that he has worked on and helped resolve. One case in particular was the Missing Spanish Girl. A Spanish girl who worked in a factory had been missing for quite a while, so her family contacted Mel and wanted to know if he could find her. He asked the family to bring her shoes and clothing to his house and also asked for an interpreter.

Through the interpreter, he explained to the parents that the girl had planned the whole thing and had run away with her boyfriend. She was alive and in Florida. He gave her boyfriend's name: John. He said John was an alcoholic and extremely abusive.

Mel saw her driving with a young man in a blue car. Soon the girl would go to the police and turn herself in. He could see bruises all over her body. He also told the parents she would be found within three weeks.

Three weeks later, the girl turned herself in to the police in Florida. She was badly bruised from the beating her boyfriend had given her. His name was John and he drove a blue car.

A Missing Child

Mel also worked on the Chala Lansing case. Six-year-old Chala was roller skating only two blocks away from her house when she disappeared suddenly.

Holding on to her clothing, Mel had a vision of the little girl; she had been murdered.

"That's the hard part, telling the family their daughter is dead." Mel sounded disturbed.

He felt Chala had been kidnapped, strangled, and then left to die. Her body would be found thirteen days after her disappearance.

Mel stated the FBI would obtain a lead through the man who kidnapped Chala. The man's name was Jeff, and he spoke with an accent. He would attempt to pick up another child. This kidnapping would fail, and the man would be turned in to the police.

Thirteen days later a man named Jeff was arrested in Missouri. Later that day he confessed to killing Chala Lansing and described where the body could be found. Chala had been strangled and left to die in a barn.

Funny Stories

The funniest story Mel could remember was about the time he was visiting his cousin Marion. While they were sitting in her dining room, Marion asked him to give her a reading. He told her he was tired. Suddenly, he didn't know what possessed him, but he looked up at her chandelier and he exclaimed, "Marion, I feel water all around you. I don't understand where this water is coming from."

The next day Marion called Mel with some startling news. "Mel, you won't believe this. After you left my apartment I went upstairs to take a bath. I ran the water and went into my bedroom. I decided to lie down for a moment. The water was filling up. I awoke to water all over the place and, of course, the water leaked through the chandelier onto my dining table where you and I were sitting yesterday. Amazing, simply amazing!"

While Mel and I were discussing this interview, I mentioned that I was going to see a Psychic surgeon from the Philippines who would be in Hawaii for just a week. I asked Mel if he believed in Psychic surgeons. His reply was "No, but, Dayle, I want you to believe."

"Why?" I asked.

"Well, let me tell you a story, dear. Many years ago I had a wart on my leg. I went to see a medical doctor and he advised me the wart should be removed. He told me it could be cancerous.

"I said, 'Well, what if it wasn't cancerous?'

"The doctor still advised that I remove the wart. I was dead set against it. I went home and fell asleep. I had a dream that I bought some wart remover. When I awoke, I ran down to the corner drugstore and bought some.

"Do you know, I opened the bottle slowly and got ready to apply the wart remover. I didn't even get the remover on my wart, when the darn thing disappeared. I believed with all my heart and soul that the wart remover was the answer to my problem. Because I believed, the wart went away.

"So you see, Dayle, the same premise applies to Psychic Surgeons. If you believe, it'll work. We all have the ability to heal ourselves. What you're doing is handing *your God-given power* to the healer. You are giving him permission to heal you."

"Very interesting, Mel," I said. "I'm still going to check out this healer."

I told Mel I'd like to end the interview with what he could see for me in the future.

"OK, are we ready?" he asked.

"Yes," I replied eagerly.

Mel's predictions for me included the following:

1. Many new national television shows.
2. Your book, *Dare to Be Different!*, will soar. I see it selling out quickly.
3. It's possible the combination of both your books, *Dare to Be Different!* and *The Psychic Within*, will be made into a two-hour television show or movie.
4. However, your third book will be extremely sought after. I see four books that you will write. Eventually, there will be a two-hour movie.
5. You will go to Europe and perform. Soon you will be internationally known on a much wider scale.
6. There will be an offer to do stage; I suggest you do it.
7. I also see you on a talk show about your book.

I thanked Mel for all the wonderful predictions. He is an outstanding Psychic with the highest code of ethics.

Ms. Beverly Lyons

Born in Hawaii on December 23, 1940, she specializes in numerology and has appeared on many radio talk shows throughout the islands. Beverly was a regular on *Night Magic,* a local Hawaii talk show on KSSK hosted by John Kealoha, and she has appeared numerous times on my show, *ESP and You.* Beverly also teaches classes in Psychic ability and numerology; she has worked in and produced many workshops and seminars.

Beverly first realized she was Psychic when she was a young girl; she would always sense when her relatives were going to die. This frightened her mother, so Beverly suppressed her ability.

I recall meeting Beverly right after my radio show on KKUA. I remember asking to meet a *kahuna*, a native Hawaiian who has healing powers. Beverly called.

"Hi, Dayle, I hear you wanted to meet a kahuna. Well, my family comes from a long line of kahunas. I would love to meet with you and trade readings."

She came to my apartment the next evening. I read for her with an accuracy that amazed even me. I told Beverly her husband would change jobs and become a truck driver. I also told her that one of her daughters would be famous. Several years later, all of this and more came to pass.

Then it was my turn. Beverly read for me and told me of my future fame. She told me I would change radio stations and my face would be known worldwide. She predicted the breakup of my first marriage (to Bob), and that some day I would come face to face with Madam Pele, the goddess of volcanoes on the Big Island of Hawaii. All Beverly predicted came to pass, including my meeting with Madam Pele, whom I was able to photograph.

Beverly was unique as a Psychic. She had the power to heal. She was caring and sensitive. I wanted to be friends with her.

I saw something special in Beverly, and I was willing to work with her and watch her potential grow. Whenever I had a television show, she was always by my side. If I had a seminar, Beverly was there.

I remember the first time she appeared with me, I practically threw her on stage. Holding her hand, I led her on stage, then let her go; there must have been 300 people in the audience. Beverly was shaking, but she did very well.

We've been friends for years and we work well together, although we don't always see eye to eye in our readings. John Kealoha named us the Dueling Psychics.

Every Psychic has a specialty; Beverly's forte is children. Whenever the topic of children comes up, I hand it right over to her. We complement each other.

Through the years, Beverly's ability increased by leaps and bounds. While working for an art gallery in Honolulu, she was able to meet and read for many movie stars.

While working on Outer Island tours, Beverly and I, with our husbands, always seem to end up on vacation together.

Beverly's predictions for me include:

1. I see your third book becoming very popular. It will be most dynamic.
2. I see you purchasing a house toward the east of where you are now.
3. There will be many national television appearances for you in the near future.
4. In later years I see you honored as a Psychic. This is a big celebration for you. I'm not there. Why am I not there?

Thank you, Beverly Lyons, for your predictions. You truly are a gifted Psychic.

This chapter has been wonderful to write. Not only have I had the pleasure to write about Psychics, but I've also had the pleasure to experience some wonderful readings.

I've found throughout the years that every Psychic needs a Psychic. It's like looking in the mirror; sometimes we can't see all our flaws.

CHAPTER 18

PSYCHIC SURGERY

The field of Psychic surgery was new to me. I'd always promised myself that if I had to have an operation I would try Psychic surgery first. Well, the Universe was providing the most opportune circumstances for me.

It all started while I was writing this book. I had quit smoking several years back and put on some weight. I decided at the beginning of the new year that I wanted to lose the weight, so I started to work out and eat sensibly.

I noticed I was feeling sluggish and fatigued. I tried exercising for several weeks, but I wasn't losing any weight. I felt something was wrong, so I went to see my doctor in Lake Tahoe.

After my physical, the doctor asked, "Have you checked your thyroid?"

I answered, "Yes, Doc, many times. In fact, when I was in Honolulu, I took a thyroid test and everything came up fine."

"Do thyroid problems run in your family?"

That question hit home. "As a matter of fact, my sister just had her thyroid removed," I said. "She had a growth on her thyroid. But it wasn't cancer or anything."

My doctor immediately asked to feel my thyroid. Then, he instructed me to get a basal thermometer. He said, "When you awake in the morning, I want you to put the thermometer under your arm for five or six minutes. Don't go to the bathroom or even move when you first get up. Mark down your body temperature for six or seven days straight. Then come back and see me.

"If your body temperature at rest is not 97.2 and above, you have a thyroid problem. You see, Dayle, we've found out that a blood test is not always accurate, but your body temperature is."

For one week straight I followed my doctor's orders. My body temperature was registering 96.5. I thought I was dead or something. I knew this wasn't normal. In fact, I thought my thermometer was broken, so I went to the drug store and bought a new one. The same thing happened. My body temperature was 96.5.

The next week I went back to the doctor and showed him my temperatures.

"Just what I suspected," he said. He reached over to touch my thyroid. "Ah! Your thyroid is swollen. I don't feel any masses or tumors. I'd like you to take this thyroid medicine."

Several weeks passed. My body temperature was almost normal, but the medicine was revving my engine just a little bit too much. The doctor decided to change my medication. I asked him if there was anything else he could do.

"We can give you a blood test and a thyroid scan," he replied.

"Okay, I want to have it done right away," I said. I went into the hospital to take the thyroid scan. They ran a gel over my thyroid and then took X-rays. When the session was over, I asked the technician if I could see the X-ray. She showed it to me. I ran my hands over the film. Although the left side of my thyroid was swollen, I didn't see or sense cancer or tumors or masses.

The technician showed the film to the radiologist. I sat in the waiting room; I knew they were going to request that I have more

X-rays. When the technician came out of the room, she told me the radiologist would be requesting my doctor to take more X-rays. Just as I thought.

That evening I went home and started to study everything I could about the thyroid. I called my sister, then my aunt. I was surprised to find out my aunt Molly had part of her thyroid removed. All these years I thought I had low blood-sugar, and now I found out it was my thyroid. I didn't know that the thyroid controls the metabolism and glucose level in one's body.

I was relieved that my doctor had found the problem. I also called several of my Psychic friends. Each and every one of them didn't see surgery. No matter how I asked the question, the answer always came back, "No cancer, no surgery."

Then I received a call from Jim, a good friend of mine in Hawaii. "Are you going to have your show in Hawaii in March?" he asked.

"I don't know, Jim," I said. "You see, I'm having problems with my thyroid. I don't know if it will be resolved in time."

Jim claimed, "You're not going to believe this, but in March there's going to be a Psychic surgeon in town! In fact, he's one of the best. Shirley MacLaine wrote about him in her book, *Going Within*. Do you want me to put you in touch with a lady who can tell you all about the surgeon?"

"Yes!" I said excitedly.

Jim called back right away. "The lady's name is Tamara. Here's her number. I told her you'll call."

I wasted no time calling Tamara. I told her of my thyroid problem.

She said, "The Psychic surgeon's name is Reverend Alex Orbito. He's from Manila. Dayle, he's wonderful. I've seen him help so many people. He's beyond belief."

"How much does he charge?" I asked.

"He charges $300 for four visits. That's how many you need to be healed," she replied. "But you must believe. If there is any negativity, it won't work. Oh, by the way, if your doctor tells you there might be surgery, please come and see Alex first. He really is remarkable."

"When will he be in town?"

"March 26 through April 2."

"Whoa! What synchronization! I can't believe it," I exclaimed. "I'm going to be in Hawaii from March 25th on."

"Well, everything happens for a reason, you know," Tamara remarked. "Why don't I set an appointment for you for on March 27th?"

"Sounds good. I'll get back to you," I said.

Meanwhile, my doctor's nurse called to say that the doctor wanted to see me in his office at five o'clock. Blythe and I were there right on time.

My doctor informed me that I had a small cyst on my thyroid. "It's the size of a pea. I don't feel it's cancer. In fact, the chances are less than one percent that it's cancer. So, I'm going to pull you off the thyroid medication." He continued, "I want you to have some nuclear testing done. You take a radiation pill, then we X-ray you, and this will tell us if the cyst is hard or soft. If it's hard, then it could be cancer, and we kill the thyroid and you continue taking medication. If it's soft, we can drain it or remove it. Sometimes it goes away with medication."

"But, Doctor, I'm supposed to go to Hawaii," I said. "I guess I can cancel my trip if I have to."

"Dayle, speaking as your doctor, I have to tell you to take the nuclear medicine. But if this were me, I would go to Hawaii and forget about it for a few months. It's possible the medication could reduce the swelling, and the cyst could disappear."

"What if I wait three months; suppose it's cancer? Will it grow real large? Would I have problems in the future?" I asked anxiously.

"No, not at all. Don't worry. Go to Hawaii," he said, trying to reassure me.

I said, "By the way, Doc, it just so happens there's going to be a Psychic surgeon in Hawaii. I'm going to try him out. When I come back, I want another test. I think this thing is going to disappear."

"That sounds exciting. I've always wanted to see one of those guys. Go for it," the doctor said.

I called Tamara and told her of my cyst. She shouted, "Don't worry, Dayle, Alex will take care of it for you, mark my words!" Synchronicity again!

Then a series of strange events started. I told my chiropractor about the Psychic surgeon and the next thing I knew, he and his wife decided to come along with me to Hawaii. The more people I told, the more people decided to come along with me. I was beginning to feel like the Pied Piper.

I was also beginning to feel a little insecure. I checked with Mel Doerr, one of my favorite Psychics.

"Don't worry, everything's going to be fine," he said. "But you know what? Something strange happened to me today. I have a client that I do free readings for, and for some unknown reason, he left me a whole bunch of medical books. I guess I'll open up the book to thyroid." Mel started to read from the book. We studied the thyroid inside and out.

"You know, Dayle, your doctor kind of did things backwards," Mel concluded. "He was supposed to give you the nuclear medicine test first, then the sonogram, way before he gave you the thyroid pills. That's why he has to take you off the medication. The nuclear test will not come up right unless you get the medication out of your system."

I said, "I know, Mel. But in the beginning, the doctor didn't want nuclear medicine going through my system. Only as a last resort would he do that. But who knows? If he did things correctly, I guess I wouldn't be seeing the Psychic surgeon."

"Now I know why these books were left on my desk," Mel commented.

"Thanks for all your help," I told Mel. "I want to research this healer a little bit more." I had seen many tapes on Psychic surgery; they have always boggled my mind. I explained to Mel that I would get in touch with Tamara and question her further about Alex Orbito.

When I questioned Tamara extensively, I found out that Alex Orbito was born on November 25, 1940, in the *barrios* of Cuyapo, Nueva Ecija, a province in the Philippines. He was not aware of his healing ability until he was 14 years old. At that age, he began to have dreams over and over of a man who said he was his spirit guide and that Alex was a great healer.

One day Alex was summoned by his mother to help a friend who was paralyzed. He went to the old woman. Without a word, he picked up a bottle of coconut oil beside her bed, massaged her legs, said a deep prayer, and commanded her to walk.

She rose from her bed for the first time in ten years and walked.

But Alex didn't want to be a healer. Strangely, the more he denied it, the sicker he became. When he used his ability, he was fine.

When I researched Shirley MacLaine's book, *Going Within,* she spoke of Alex very highly. She witnessed Alex do several surgeries a day. Most of them took from one minute to twenty minutes.

She watched the most amazing things happen to people. He actually opened up the body of one of her friends and put her hand along with his inside of her friend's chest. Most amazing.

Now it was my turn to witness this most remarkable man who claims God heals and he doesn't. Alex says he is only an instrument of God.

So I decided it was time to go back to the Islands, time to experience what Shirley MacLaine has known all along, but this time I wouldn't be alone. My husband Blythe wanted to experience the Psychic healer as well. Blythe had a cystic growth on his left wrist that he wanted removed.

Then there was my chiropractor Don and his wife Lorna, who were just plain curious. Although Don had heard of Psychic healers before, he wanted to experience Alex's ability first hand. While practicing as a chiropractor, Don developed a degeneration in his back; he wanted to see if the Psychic surgeon could help him.

So off we went on another adventure, one that would open my eyes to a brighter future.

Blythe and I arrived in Hawaii on March 23, 1993. That particular week was one big whirlwind. I was preparing for my show, *ESP & You,* which would air live on March 30th. In the meantime, we were patiently awaiting the arrival of my chiropractor and his wife.

Don and Lorna arrived the next day; now our journey would begin. We were excited and jubilant. I had approximately four days to get my healing done, then I would film my television show. I had so much faith in this man. I knew in my heart he would heal my thyroid and make the nodule disappear.

Bright and early the next morning Don, Blythe and I headed for the Plantation Spa in Kaaawa where our healings would begin. Lorna was somewhat of a skeptic; she decided to stay home and soak up the rays. We were told beforehand that we must remain positive, or the healings would not work. We could not allow any negativity around us. After a two-hour drive, we arrived at the plantation. There were many cars in the parking lot, and since this was our first visit, we didn't know what to expect. We followed the road by foot to the main entrance of the plantation. There we were greeted by Tamara.

She said, "Hi, Dayle, so nice to meet you in person. We've been waiting for you and your guests. Why don't you have a seat. While you are waiting, you can pay the lady in white at the counter and Alex will be with you shortly. We need you and your friends to fill out this form. On the form, list at least three things you need healed."

I looked down a hall and saw a long line of people. There seemed to be at least sixty people on the grounds waiting to see Alex. We sat down and chatted with the rest of the people until we were called. The line to see Alex was beginning to grow even longer.

I was nervous. Our turn was next. We were ushered to the front of the line. I realized I was going to be first to enter the room. I began to hyperventilate.

"Don, you go first," I insisted. Don entered the room. About one minute later he reappeared outside. "Dayle, it's amazing! Unbelievable!" he shouted. "Nothing to be scared of; it's painless."

I mustered up enough nerve to enter the room. I walked slowly. A lady in a white outfit ushered me into the room. There sat Alex Orbito. I was in awe. He was wearing a white uniform just like a doctor's. I noticed there was a twin-sized bed in the room and Alex sat behind the bed with his hands folded. Next to Alex was a trash can. I noticed no surgical instruments of any kind.

The lady, who was Alex Orbito's wife, asked me to lie down on the bed. I was fully clothed. She told me to relax. I obeyed. I wasn't frightened anymore; for some reason I felt at peace with myself. Mrs. Orbito read out loud what I had written on the piece of paper. "Thyroid. And pain in left shoulder of arm. Pain in the lower and upper back," she said. Alex nodded.

I closed my eyes. I didn't want to see what Alex was doing. I felt his fingers scratch my neck. It seemed his fingers were penetrating my throat. Then I felt his fingers enter my throat. It seemed as though they were sloshing around inside of my neck exactly where the thyroid nodule was. Within moments, Alex demanded that I open my eyes. I did. He extracted a blood clot, which I believed came from my thyroid, and held this clot right before my eyes.

"See," Alex said.

"Whoa!" I said. Then I was asked to leave the room. They were ready for the next person. I walked out of the room very light-headed, almost as if I were floating. One of his helpers sat me down and asked me to drink water. I was definitely floating. "What an experience." It only took a moment.

Out of the corner of my eye I saw Blythe enter the room. Moments later he was out. Blythe came over to me. "Are you all right?" he asked.

"Yes," I responded. "How about you? Let me see your hand. Is the cyst gone?" Blythe showed me his left hand. The cyst appeared much smaller in size. "Whoa!" I was excited.

We all gathered together, Don, Blythe, and I. We had to get back to the house. Our next healing would be tomorrow.

On the way home, we kept chattering; we couldn't contain ourselves. Don felt wonderful; he was free of pain for the first time in many years. I felt good, but I kept wondering why Alex didn't remove Blythe's cyst altogether. Although the cyst was smaller in size, I wondered why he couldn't just pluck it out. Don reminded me this was only our first healing. I gave Don the benefit of a doubt.

We had been handed a sheet of paper explaining to us why we should not discuss this operation with anyone. We were asked to wait twenty-one days after the healing before we discussed this with any nonbelievers. Alex felt the more people we discussed this with, the more energy we would lose. We were supposed to contain ourselves and keep the healing inside of ourselves.

Don was very impressed with Alex. Blythe felt good about the operation. I felt as though he had removed the nodule from my thyroid. I would wait the twenty-one days before I checked with my doctor to scan my thyroid.

When we returned to the house, Lorna asked how everything went. We told her we couldn't discuss the matter. Lorna felt hurt. Don proceeded to explain why, but Lorna was still hurt. She mumbled, "Well, I don't believe in those things anyway."

Day two. Back to the plantation. We arrived at the plantation around noon, eager to experience another healing. We were greeted by Tamara and ushered into the room promptly.

This time I was the first one to enter the room. Alex smiled. This time as I lay on the table, Alex took his time and worked on me for an exceptionally long period. It seemed as though once he found out I was a writer, the time he spent with me was extremely thorough. I was impressed. But I sensed an uneasiness about him; he seemed extremely tense. Before long, Alex pulled out another mass of clots from my thyroid. I was pleased. I explained to him I was having severe pain in my left shoulder from a fall I had taken in Lake Tahoe. Alex worked hard on my shoulder, but the pain seemed to intensify. Alex smiled when the session was over, and I was asked to leave the room.

Tamara asked me to stick around after the healings, for Alex wanted to speak to me. He accepted my offer to interview him for this book, and he also wanted a reading.

Don was the next patient. He seemed to be in the room for a long period of time. When he came out, he was smiling once again. Blythe was next. Blythe came and went. I asked him if I could look at his cyst. It seemed to be shrinking. I was pleased. I decided to interview several of the other patients while waiting to see Alex again.

One of my friends, Kat, was there. She had been in a serious car accident and she wanted Alex to heal her back. I asked her how she felt. Kat responded, "Dayle, I never felt better in my whole life. This man is truly amazing."

Time passed. Tamara told us Alex had fewer people than expected, so he would go ahead with our third healing. Each healing was quick and fast.

After Alex had seen his last patient, Blythe and I met with Alex in his healing room, where the interview would take place.

"What exactly are you going to write about Psychic surgery?" he asked.

"I thought I would write about my experience with Psychic surgery and what it felt like," I replied.

"I understand," he said.

I looked deep into Alex's eyes and realized he was frightened about something. What that something was, I didn't know. Maybe I wasn't healed; maybe he was scared of what I would say. I continued with the interview.

I paused for a moment. "Alex, may I hold on to something you wear? I would like to give you a reading." He complied.

I said. "Alex, I see you are worried about not making enough money." He shook his head and nodded downward. "Don't worry, enough people will come. I see you were very poor at one time, and you came from nothing. I also see you want to build a center for healing."

Alex perked up and came alive. "Dayle, you are right. I have this dream. I want to help the people of my country with a healing center. How did you know that? I don't know where I'm going to get the money."

"Don't worry, Alex, I know the money will come." And I meant that sincerely. The reading went on for a while. Alex seemed very pleased. Then I returned to the interview.

"Alex, who do you go to when you get sick? I mean, who heals you?"

"I've never been to a doctor. God heals me," he answered.

"What does it feel like when you are working on someone?"

"I don't know. I remove myself from the situation. God is working through me."

"Why are there so many Psychic surgeons from the Philippines?" I asked.

"I feel the Philippines is a very special place. We believe in God very strongly," He answered.

"You mean in order to be healed, you have to believe?"

"It helps. The stronger you believe, the more you will be healed. You see, that stuff I take from your body is not of human nature; it's what you would call negative energy. If I went into your body and came up with nothing, you wouldn't believe. The healing process would not begin. In order to be healed, I must show you the negativity that has come from your body so that you will believe," he said.

"I understand. If we can see it, we will believe it," I said. "I guess you can heal without going into the body."

"Yes, exactly," he said.

I pointed to my husband's hand and the cyst. "You mean this will go away?"

Alex nodded.

"Alex, can I watch you operate?" I asked.

"Yes, you can. We'll use your husband."

I called Don to come into the room. We sat in silence as Blythe lay on the twin bed. Within moments, Don and I were amazed. We watched Alex pop two fingers into the middle of Blythe's stomach. We saw this with our own eyes. There appeared to be no trickery of any kind. As we watched in awe, Alex plunged his fist into Blythe's stomach and sloshed his hand around in the open wound. Don and I stared in amazement. Alex's fist and hand were invisible, well within Blythe's stomach. I couldn't believe my eyes. Yet Blythe felt nothing. Then Alex prayed for a moment, and the wound closed.

Next, Alex asked a woman to enter the room. He asked her to lie on the bed while his wife ushered in several onlookers. As all watched, he plunged his fingers right smack into the middle of this woman's stomach.

Alex motioned for me to stand next to him. Alex's left hand was fully submerged into the woman's stomach. His right hand reached out and grabbed my hand. Alex held my hand and placed it with his, and we both closed the wound on the woman's stomach together. What an experience! I remember leaving in awe.

Day three. We each had received three healings; now we were to experience the fourth. We headed to a donated office somewhere in town. There must have been at least one hundred people waiting and sitting around on the floor. Once again we were ushered to the front of the line and healed promptly. This would be the last time I would see Alex for healings. That evening Tamara called and asked me to attend Alex's lecture as his guest.

I found out that Alex's lectures were separate from his healings. The price was $300 for a series of four lectures. There were many people that evening asking questions, all wanting to understand what Alex did. I listened to the lecture and decided to ask Alex a question of my own. "What happens when you submerge your hands into a patient who has AIDS; will you catch it?" I asked.

Alex responded, "Dayle, that is a good question. But since God is working through me, I will not get AIDS."

The meeting ended. Alex whispered in my ear he wanted to meet with me. He felt some way we could help each other. He told me he would call me and that we should get together.

The next day I was unable to attend the meeting with Alex,

so Don went in my place. I did receive a message from Alex on my recorder that he wanted to get in touch with me as soon as possible.

When Don came home, he informed me that Alex was rushed to a plane and was well on his way to the Philippines. Someone had reported Alex for practicing medicine without a license.

I thoroughly enjoyed my meeting with Alex. It was worth the $300 just to watch him perform. Twenty-one days passed. Don and Lorna were back in Lake Tahoe. Now I would know the truth about Alex's ability.

I set up an appointment with a doctor who specializes in thyroid problems. I was anxious. I explained to the doctor about the Psychic surgeon. Of course, he was skeptical. Now it was time to test Alex Orbito. I underwent another thyroid scan, and within an hour I had my results. The nodule was still there the same size; nothing had changed. The doctor commented, "I guess it didn't work."

I must say I was disappointed. I was even more disappointed for my husband; his cyst still appeared on his hand, although for a short period, the cyst had reduced itself in size.

I wanted to give Alex the benefit of the doubt. I waited for seven more months before I retested my thyroid again in Hawaii. I thought maybe, just maybe, I didn't give the situation enough time. Seven months later, my thyroid nodule had not grown in size; in fact, the nodule had shrunk a tad. But I did notice a change in myself. I felt better than I have ever felt in my whole life. My husband Blythe experienced no change. Doctor Don felt wonderful. And my friend Kat felt great as well.

I really wanted to believe in this man. You see, I had been to healers before, and whatever problems I had were cured. This included going to a Rabbi in North Carolina at a time when I had three bad pap smears and surgery was suggested. After the visit with the healing Rabbi, my body returned to normal.

In the depths of my heart, I believe certain healers are gifted. And only God knows I've been to many of them. I felt Alex was a good healer, but at the same time money was his first love. He seemed to have very little compassion for each individual. I'm sure there have been many people whom Alex has helped at one time or another. But, in this instance, I was not cured, and neither was my husband. I can only go by what had occurred to me and my family.

But my chiropractor will swear by him, and my friend Kat feels the same way. I can't argue with them. I can teach people only to judge for themselves.

I didn't disbelieve Alex; that wasn't my problem. I believed in him too much.

CHAPTER 19

IMELDA MARCOS

When Imelda and Ferdinand Marcos escaped from the Philippines and arrived in Hawaii, all hell broke loose. Reporters followed them about endlessly. The Marcoses were the topic of conversation nationwide, constantly in the news and battling for their lives. Hardly a day went by without their names being mentioned in some unkindly way.

Several years later, the Marcoses were living in upper Maikiki an exclusive area in Honolulu. I never paid much attention to their family; however, all that would change.

Early one evening I received a phone call from my friend Beverly Lyons, the fine Psychic. She said, "You're not going to believe this; I went to a party at the Marcoses' house the other night. I can't believe I actually saw Imelda and Mr. Marcos."

"That must have been exciting. What was she like?" I asked.

"She's charming and down to earth," Bev replied. "Do you want to meet her? I can arrange it through one of her friends."

"Yes, I do," I said with anticipation. "I mean, a President and his wife; I never met anyone so important."

"Don't worry, Dayle. I'll take care of it and call you in a few days."

I was excited. I couldn't wait to see Mrs. Marcos. I was interested and curious about where she got her 3000 pairs of shoes. I had so many questions in my mind, my head was spinning.

A few evenings later Bev called. "Dayle, get ready; we're invited to see Mrs. Marcos."

"Bev, are you serious?" I said, trying to sound calm.

"Well, Dayle, if you want to see Mrs. Marcos, you'd better hurry. We're supposed to meet in this parking lot next to a restaurant. Then someone will park next to us and we'll switch cars."

I was confused. I asked Bev, "Why are we switching cars? This sounds like a movie plot."

"Dayle, don't worry. Why don't you hurry; I'll meet you at the restaurant in about twenty minutes."

Shortly thereafter, I arrived at the restaurant and we made the switch. I remember sitting in the back seat of a sedan. We seemed to drive endlessly up this road. Finally, the car stopped; we got out and someone parked our car. There were several guards at the entrance of the Marcos' house.

My heart was pounding. Bev and I walked down a long driveway which led to the entrance of her house. The doors were flung open and we slowly walked in. There were people all over the place, dancing and celebrating; music was playing. We were told to have some food and mingle.

"Bev, what's going on?"

"I guess it's a party of some kind."

In the background I could hear a language I was unfamiliar with. Bev explained that the people who worked for the Marcoses spoke Filipino.

I saw Mr. and Mrs. Marcos on stage, singing. I couldn't believe my eyes. I can't explain what it felt like to see them; they looked like characters out of a movie. I felt strange. You know the feeling—when someone you've seen on television for years all of a sudden comes to life right before your eyes.

The room was filled with people from all walks of life. I found out later that many of them were Filipino supporters and friends of the President and his wife. The celebration went on.

Bev explained that the food that we were eating was different from what the Marcoses ate. They had to be careful; apparently, they were fearful someone might poison them. So, the chefs prepared special dishes for the Marcoses.

"Oh, great, Bev. What you're telling me is we're her guinea pigs. I don't think I want anything to eat, thank you," I remarked.

Bev laughed. "Don't worry, Dayle, they're not going to poison us."

The hours passed rather quickly. Mr. and Mrs. Marcos sang song after song. Every so often there would be an outburst from Imelda. "Soon we'll be in the Philippines," she would exclaim. "Víva la Philippines!"

It was getting late. "Bev, I think it's time to go home," I said.

"But, Dayle, you haven't met Mrs. Marcos."

"Don't worry; I'll meet her in the future," I assured Bev.

We asked for a driver to take us back to our cars. During the ride, Bev and I discussed how exciting it had been. I couldn't believe we had been in Imelda Marcos' house and had gotten to see her.

After we thanked the driver for dropping us off at our cars, I told Bev that I would call her the next day and made my way home.

The next night the phone rang; Bev was on the line. "Dayle, Mrs. Marcos wants to meet us personally. She wants you and me to come up and give her a reading."

"Now!"

"Yes, she felt bad that she couldn't speak with us because of her party, so she wants us to come up now."

"Bev, it's kind of late. I mean, it's eleven o'clock at night."

"Well, it's up to you; I'm going," Bev said proudly.

That got me riled. "I'm going, too. Where do we meet?"

"At the same restaurant. There will be a car waiting for us."

"Can I bring Blythe this time?" I asked.

"I don't see why not," Bev replied. "Bring him; we don't want him to miss out."

I said, "By the way, Bev, I'm worried about something."

"What?"

"Well, you know I never get involved with political people. What if something comes down? You know what I mean. And besides, I don't want to do anything against our government's wishes. I'm sure her house is being bugged by the feds. What do you think?" I was a bit nervous.

"I know what you mean, Dayle. But what harm can there be in us giving her a reading?" Bev didn't sound concerned at all.

"I guess you're right. I'll see you within the hour at the restaurant." I hung up the phone and shouted, "Blythe, get ready; were going to meet Mrs. Marcos! Here we go again."

We were off and running. We met Mrs. Marcos' car at the restaurant and proceeded to her home in upper Maikiki. This time we were greeted by Mrs. Marcos herself at the door.

"Come in. You must be Dayle Schear, the famous Psychic I've been hearing about. And, of course, I know Bev. Welcome to my home," she said warmly.

I introduced Mrs. Marcos to my husband, and Mr. Marcos came down briefly and introduced himself.

Since it was getting late, Mrs. Marcos asked if I would mind giving her a reading first. I sent Blythe with her into her room to explain how I work. The reading was to be done in her bedroom—an unusual place, but I was willing.

I was nervous as she took her HUGE diamond ring off her finger and handed it to me.

"Mrs. Marcos, I never know if I'm in the past, present or the future when I am rattling on. If I'm in the past, please let me know," I said.

She nodded. "Please go on."

I held her ring tightly in my hands. Within moments the visions came.

Mrs. Marcos sat in silence throughout the reading.

Transcript of the Marcos' reading:

> I don't want you to worry; everything is going to be all right. I see legalities surrounding you. There seems to be a court trial, but you will win. (Mrs. Marcos won her court trial in the United States.) I see Mr. Marcos is not in good health. He will pass on. I don't know when.
>
> You have to understand you won't be allowed to go to the Philippines until your husband's passing. I'm sorry to tell you this, but your husband will never see his homeland while he is alive.
>
> I see you in New York for some reason.
>
> There will be many books written about you. And I see a movie being made about your life. Men will honor you later in life.
>
> You have had much sorrow in your life, and there is more to come. At the end you will get your wish; you will be able to live in the Philippines.

Mrs. Marcos asked me questions about her family. I answered. I, in turn, asked if she remembered my teacher, Peter Hurkos. At one time she had summoned him to come to the Philippines and read for her. She remembered him and asked how he was doing.

After the reading, she seemed quite pleased. She piercingly stared at me and said, "You know, Dayle, you're very good."

"Thank you," I said, smiling.

Beverly was next. She retired into the room of Mrs. Marcos and read her for about twenty minutes. When the readings were over, Mrs. Marcos asked us to join her in the backyard and showed us around the grounds.

The land her house was sitting on was unbelievable. She had a spectacular, panoramic view of Honolulu. To the left of her property was a little temple with a statue of the Virgin Mother Mary and Jesus. She was proud of her worshiping place.

We sat down at a very large picnic table; there must have been thirty people who joined us for food and story-telling.

I asked Mrs. Marcos how she had met her husband. She told me that when she was a young girl she saw him in passing and fell deeply in love with him. They started dating and it turned into a wonderful marriage. She talked proudly about the several beautiful children she had with him.

She also talked a lot about the Philippines' President, Corey Aquino. Was there jealousy between the two? Mrs. Marcos spent hours telling us how much she herself had done for her country. However, since I was not in the political arena, most of what she explained was unfamiliar to me.

Although I realized differently, she claimed she was penniless, since our government had frozen most of her assets. She introduced us to several influential Filipino ladies who had come to the United States to stay with her and help her out financially.

I asked Mrs. Marcos the burning question that had been on my mind. "How did the story start about your shoes?"

She answered without hesitating. "Well, in my country, Mr. Marcos and myself have helped many people start their business. We gave them enough money to begin a new life. Many of these businesses were clothing stores and such. So, whenever I went shopping over the years, I would shop in my friends' stores and give them business. They were so grateful that I was shopping there, they always asked if I wanted anything. I love shoes. So over the years of shopping they handed me several pairs of shoes for free. I had no idea there were 3,000, and till this day I'll never believe there were that many."

As for the allegations that Mrs. Marcos had an account somewhere in the United States worth well over $700,000, she brought up the subject herself. She explained that when her children were little, she started a fund for them, put a small amount of money in the bank at a high interest rate, then forgot about the account. Twenty years later, our government found the account and the accumulated interest. That's how $700,000 appeared in one of her accounts, she said.

Very interesting, I thought. Well, before we knew it, it was four o'clock in the morning. I didn't realize we were so engrossed in listening to Mrs. Marcos; she was so fascinating. Although she wanted to keep talking, I had to interrupt her.

"Sorry, Mrs. Marcos, it's getting late and we all have to work in the morning," I said.

"Well, thanks for coming, Dayle. I hope you can join me again in the future." She walked us to the door and thanked us again for coming.

"By the way, Dayle, who do you think the next President will be?" she asked. We were approaching the election and Ronald Reagan was finishing his second term as President.

"I think Bush will win," I said.

"So do I!" Mrs. Marcos interjected.

We said our good-byes. Throughout the drive home I kept reflecting on that once-in-a-lifetime evening. I couldn't believe how eloquent she was. She had charm and charisma. I felt sorry for anyone who would go up against her, for surely she would win.

In her heart she believed that whatever she did for her country was for the best. She could not see the poverty or sickness. She only saw the good that Mr. Marcos and she achieved.

Within a year, Mr. Marcos died. She built a tomb for him in Hawaii and kept him on ice, believing that one day she will be able to bring him back to his country to rest in peace.

As for her future, Mrs. Marcos did stand trial in the United States and won, just as I had predicted. She now lives in the Philippines; I wouldn't be surprised if she gains power once again.

Because I'm not into politics and know very little about the situation in the Philippines, I refuse to take sides. Many people are against the Marcoses and many people are for them. All I can say about meeting Mrs. Marcos is that it was an experience of a lifetime for me.

CHAPTER 20

A BIZARRE REQUEST

The phone rang while I was typing this book.

"Hello."

"Hi, Dayle, this is Rob Nikoleski, sports anchor for Channel 8 KOLO News. How are you at predicting basketball games?"

I sat in silence on the phone for a moment. Then I heard the urgency in Rob's voice. I knew he wasn't joking. "Rob, I've never predicted sports before," I said.

This is different," he insisted. "This is our Wolf Pack team. They've lost *ten* straight games in a row. Isn't there anything you can do?"

"Well, this certainly is a bizarre request," I said.

"What do you mean? What kind of requests do you normally get?" he asked.

"Oh, sometimes I'm asked to find a missing person. Sometimes I'm asked to find a murder victim. Mostly, I concentrate on helping people straighten out their lives," I replied. "To tell you the truth, I know very little about basketball, and I've had very little experience with sports."

"Oh, I see," he said. "But can't you do something? I mean, if I gave you something of the basketball team, could you tell us how they can improve? On a serious note, Dayle, I just want them to win. The coach has resorted to having the team take showers together to wash some of the unluckiness off of them; now, I think that's bizarre. That's when I came up with the idea of a Psychic trying to help the team."

If it weren't for the seriousness in Rob's voice, I probably would have turned him down. I knew this team meant a lot to him for some reason. I decided to approach this situation in a different way. "Rob, I think I can help. I'll take a look at the videotape of the team and see how I can give the players some positive feedback."

Robs voice perked up. "That sounds great, Dayle. That's all we want you to do. I'll call you in a few days."

As I hung up, Blythe shouted from the other room, "Dayle, what did Rob want?"

I shouted back, "It seems there's a basketball team in Reno who are on a losing streak, and Rob wants me to analyze the team and tell him what I see." I went back to writing my book.

Blythe came rushing into my office. "What? That's crazy! I've never heard of such a thing. Can you help them, Dayle?"

"I don't know, Blythe, but I can try. I feel sorry for him," I said.

Ordinarily, I would never take a case like this. I don't believe in predictions for gambling of any kind. This was different; gambling wasn't involved. I was going to analyze the team. I felt comfortable with my decision.

Several days passed before I heard from Rob. "Hi, Dayle, we have the crew. Can we film you tomorrow?"

"Sure," I said.

I decided to call our local paper, *The Tahoe Tribune*. I asked for the sports department and got connected with Steve Yingling, *Tribune* sports editor. I explained my story to Steve and asked if he'd like to cover the story.

"Dayle, this is bizarre. I never heard of anyone asking a Psychic to help a basketball team win. This is different. Sure, I'll come up," Steve said.

At eleven o'clock the next morning, everyone arrived. I had the reporter asking me questions, and Rob was there with his crew. I couldn't understand why everyone was making such a fuss over a basketball team.

Lights! Camera! Action! Rob handed me the shorts of Kirk Davidson, a junior reserve basketball player on the team. Rob put on a video of the Wolf Pack team and I watched them play. "What's the matter with them!" I shouted. "They're not focused. They're like an unguided missile. They're not hungry enough. They have the potential to win, but they seem defeated before they start. The other team is taking the ball away from them, just like they would take candy from a baby."

Rob seemed to enjoy what I was saying. He asked me several questions about the team. Then came the big question: "Dayle, the team has four games left before the end of the season. Do you think they can win?"

Without realizing what I was saying, I blurted out, "I wouldn't be surprised if they *won their next game.* I'm going to send a lot of positive energy tomorrow night. They're going to win *within* the next four games, that's for sure." The interview was over.

That evening Blythe and I turned on the six o'clock news. Rob promoted me like hell. "Well, folks, tune in tomorrow and find out if Dayle and the Wolf Pack will be the grand winner. We're all rooting for you, Dayle."

Oh my god, I went out on the limb without even knowing what I had said. I actually predicted the Wolf Pack would win tomorrow.

I didn't realize how important this team was to the state of Nevada. Oh well, I had a lot of praying to do.

The next evening I paced. I realized the importance of my prediction. The Wolf Pack was playing in Reno against San Jose State. I called our local radio station during the halftime to find out what the score was. The Wolf Pack was trailing by six points. I thought to myself, "No! This can't happen. They have to win." I started concentrating. I visualized the Wolf Pack winning. Then I let go of the vision.

Several hours later the phone rang. It was Rob calling to tell me the Wolf Pack had broken their loosing streak. They won 68 to 64 against San Jose. I was overjoyed, to say the least. I thanked Rob. He asked me if he could interview me the next day for the news.

"Yes," I replied giddily.

"Oh, by the way, Dayle, don't forget to watch the news at eleven," he said.

Blythe and I turned on the news. There I was. The whole Wolf Pack team and the coach were paying tribute to this Psychic.

The following article appeared in *The Tahoe Tribune,* Friday, February 18, 1993.

South Shore Psychic Picks on the Pack

Written by Steve Yingling

Schear called upon to predict when Nevada will win another game.

A Psychic/author who claims to know little about basketball has the answer all of Northern Nevada is waiting for.

When will the University of Nevada men's basketball team win again?

Dayle Schear of Kingsbury didn't know there was a pack of wolves in Reno suffering through a 10-game losing streak until she received a phone call from Sports Director Rob Nikoleski of KOLO News Station 8 last week.

In recent years, Schear has become widely known for helping solve homicide investigations with her psychometry ability. By touching personal possessions like jewelry, glasses or clothing, Schear says she can foretell someone's future or events of their past.

Having never worked on a sports-related case before, Schear was caught off guard by Nikoleski's request to predict Nevada's next win for his viewers.

"I thought it was a bizarre request," said Schear from her home on Wednesday afternoon. "I'm not into sports, and I don't know anything about basketball."

Ice skating is the only sport Schear claims to be versed in.

Nikoleski brought Schear the uniform shorts of junior reserve Kirk Davidson and a tape of the Pack's 81-69 loss to Pacific on Monday night.

Nikoleski said he came up with the idea to enlist in a Psychic after Nevada coach Len Stevens divulged that he had his team shower together in hopes of washing away the losses.

After viewing a portion of the Pacific defeat, Schear had a few suggestions for Stevens.

"It's not my team, but if I was the coach I would want them to try hypnotherapy, watch inspirational films like *Rocky*, and become more focused," said Schear, who recently released her first book, *Dare to Be Different!*

"The other team knows they can beat these guys."

By "Schear" chance, the South Shore Psychic offered a prediction as to when the Pack will be back in the win column.

"I wouldn't be surprised if they won their next game," she predicted. "I'm going to send a lot of positive energy out (to-

> night). They are going to win within the next four games, that's for sure."
>
> The Wolf Pack's best chance to end its losing ways will come tonight when it entertains 6-13 San Jose State. After that, Nevada concludes its season with three tough road games at UNLV, New Mexico State and Utah State.
>
> Nevada can only hope that Schear's energy is on the mark.

What a tribute for such a small feat, I thought. Oh, but it gets better! The next evening, the KOLO News Channel 8 team interviewed the coach. His words will forever remain in my heart.

"Coach, what do you think about what our Psychic said about your team?" Rob asked.

"We were all fired up when we heard the Psychic speak," the coach said. "Well, to tell you the truth, I never thought of using a Psychic before. We've tried everything else, but who can argue with the supernatural?"

Then player Kirk Davidson was interviewed. "How do you feel about a Psychic holding your shorts?"

Kirk replied, "Whatever it takes. You can bring my shorts up to her anytime you want—if it will make us win."

The coached muttered, "We have to find this lady. Next week we're going to play in Las Vegas and we want to win. By the way, Rob, I notice my boys are more positive now."

The Channel 8 News team closed the program and thanked me for what I had done.

This article appeared in *The Tahoe Tribune,* Sunday, February 21, 1993.

Schear Luck?

By Steve Yingling

Did the Wolf Pack end its long losing streak on its own Thursday night, or did local Psychic/author Dayle Schear play a part?

The University of Nevada men's basketball team ended a 10-game losing streak with a 68-64 triumph over San Jose State in Reno. A day earlier, Schear told a Reno TV sports director that the Pack would likely win its next game or end its tailspin before playing out its final four games.

"I called the (TV station) at halftime and found out they were losing, so I really started concentrating and did the best I could," Schear said.

It marked the first time that Schear had used her psychometry ability to make a prediction in sports.

"I think I'll rest with one victory unless they offer me a tremendous amount of money to be a team mascot," she said.

All I can say is, what a tribute! I never knew there was so much fame in sports. All these years I've worked long and hard for the police and families finding dead bodies. Never in my career had I ever been praised; this was the first time—and all this for helping a basketball team win a game. The news clip from Channel 8 KOLO was made available to over 358 national ABC affiliate stations.

How bizarre!

CHAPTER 21

LIVING WITH A PSYCHIC
as told by Blythe Arakawa

> *Since my husband knows me better than anyone in the world, I decided that he should write a chapter about me for this book. Here it is.*

Since my wife is a Psychic, I'm always asked the same questions repeatedly: "How did you meet Dayle? What is it like to live with a Psychic? Doesn't it bother you that she can read your mind?"

I always smile at the persons who ask me these questions and say, "When you have nothing to hide, you have nothing to worry about."

All in all, life with a Psychic is very interesting and exciting. There's never a dull moment. Just when you think things are peaceful, within a moment your whole world can be turned upside down.

The life-style of a Psychic is very erratic. The emotions of the Psychic are like riding a roller coaster: there are extreme highs and extreme lows. Life changes very abruptly for a Psychic, almost right before your eyes. She can be happy one moment and sad the next. You never know what to expect.

I've known my wife for about eight years. I've experienced all the rides, the changes of seasons and more. With her I find life to be a lot more exciting, because I never know what's going to happen next.

Although I first heard of Dayle on the radio, our first meeting was when I was promoting singer-songwriter Audy Kimura. Our paths crossed constantly; whenever Audy had an appearance, Dayle always seemed to be on the same show. We became the best of friends, since we had so much in common.

On several occasions Dayle asked me to help her career, but I was involved with helping Audy with his career. I wanted to help her, but I was much too busy.

Years later on my way back from London, I stopped in Oakland, then drove to Sacramento to spend a few days with my cousin. I remember Dave Lancaster, Dayle's radio deejay, telling me she was appearing at Harrah's in Lake Tahoe.

Since Sacramento is only 99 miles from Lake Tahoe, on the spur of the moment I jumped into my car to pay Dayle a visit. It was 9:00 p.m. I drove through a blizzard with zero visibility. Five minutes before Dayle was to perform, there I was, sitting in the audience in the back row. Dayle recognized me and smiled.

After the show, she asked me to spend the night, for the weather was hazardous. We stayed up all night watching movies and talking endlessly. Dayle asked me to try to get her a new radio gig in Hawaii. Before I left Lake Tahoe, I promised I would find a radio spot for her in Hawaii. As fate would have it, I got Dayle a regular spot on KSSK radio, and I've been on that wild, zany roller coaster ride ever since.

One of my first adventures with Dayle was playing golf in Alaska at ten o'clock in the evening. Of course, the sun never sets in Alaska till midnight. I remember we were on the fourth hole at Elmendorf Air Force Base golf course. I was enjoying a peaceful round of golf, when Dayle bent down and picked up a tee that belonged to the foursome in front of us.

She threw the tee in the air and screamed, "Those guys are murderers! Don't you dare hit your ball into them!"

"So much for the peaceful round of golf," I groaned.

I've also noticed that Psychics have very vivid dreams. They seem to recall every little detail of their zany, wild dreams.

My wife has this habit of constantly waking me up at one, two, three or four o'clock in the morning just to tell me her dreams—like I really want to know at four in the morning.

She also has an uncanny ability to have out-of-body experiences. On one particular late, late night I was sound asleep when Dayle suddenly woke me up.

"Blythe, I hear music. Don't you hear it?"

"I don't hear anything," I mumbled sleepily.

"It sounds like a rock and roll station. It's so loud!" Dayle exclaimed.

I responded, "Why don't you change the station? What are you listening to, K-G-O-D?"

"What?"

"The radio station you must be listening to; it must be K-God." We both laughed and fell back to sleep.

Another adventure with Dayle happened while we were living in the Bay Area. She was appearing on the television show, *AM San Francisco,* and we were working seven days a week. After a few weeks I felt we needed some time off, so we decided to take a nice drive down the coast to Santa Cruz. The ride along the coast and through the mountains was overwhelmingly beautiful.

Three hours later we made it to Santa Cruz. As soon as we entered the town, Dayle seemed nervous and jumpy. She shouted,

"I want to go home!" Her outburst startled me. "Why do you want to go home? We just got here."

"Blythe, I'm picking up strange feelings in this area. It's not safe to be here. I'm picking up runaways and murder." She insisted, "I want to go home!"

I convinced her to at least go for a walk on the pier.

"What's so threatening here?" I wondered. I was enjoying the scenery and wanted to explore the amusement park. It seemed so nice and peaceful.

Dayle's perception and mine were different. Psychics are feelers; she was definitely feeling and sensing all the anger, abusiveness and despair of the people in the town. She saw what had gone on in the past with the people of Santa Cruz as well as what would take placed in the future. I, on the other hand, saw only the visual aspects and the beauty of Santa Cruz.

Dayle felt there were a lot of teenage runaways in town. They didn't know where their next meal was coming from. They didn't know where they were going to sleep at night.

She could feel their poverty and the anxiety of the people in Santa Cruz. Later we found out that Santa Cruz was one of the runaway capitals in the United States. What I thought would be a four-hour relaxation period for us abruptly ended in twenty minutes.

I understood her feelings very well. Sometimes Psychics pick up energy that we, as "normal" people, can never understand. Dayle could see beyond the beauty that was visible all over Santa Cruz. She could sense danger.

I must say we did have a beautiful ride back to San Francisco, through the mountains and up the coast, until Dayle came to herself.

Might I also mention, it's so much fun to fly with a Psychic; it's an experience in itself. Every flight that has been planned ends up in chaos.

There was the time we were about fly back to San Francisco from Newark, New Jersey. We sat comfortably in our seats in first class. Just as we were about to take off, the pilot announced we were having engine trouble and there would be a thirty-minute delay.

That was it! My Psychic wife picked up her purse and headed out the door. I turned around to an empty seat. Where did she go?

"Blythe, come on, we're getting out of here!" she snapped.

Well, to make a long story short, Dayle argued with the flight attendant until she let us off the plane. We re-rented a car and re-rented a hotel room and caught a flight the next day. The whole time my wife was on the phone with the airlines just to prove the point that we would have missed all our connecting flights.

Then there was the time we were in Alaska, boarding our flight for Hawaii. My wife has a strange thing about resetting her watch just before we fly. She always wants to be in the same time zone as where we are heading.

Dayle once told me that if her watch won't turn backward or forwards, we won't be flying anywhere. Boy, was she right! I couldn't reset her watch on that Alaska to Hawaii flight, so I gave up. The plane took off. About an hour into the flight, the pilot's voice came over the loud speaker: "Sorry, folks, we're having manifold problems; we have to turn back to Anchorage." My wife was right again.

She also believes that when a plane has problems, one should take another flight. So, naturally, when the plane landed and the

BLUE DOLPHIN PUBLISHING, INC.
Mailing List
P.O. Box 1920
Nevada City, CA 95959-1920

PLACE
POSTCARD
STAMP
HERE

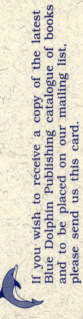

If you wish to receive a copy of the latest Blue Dolphin Publishing catalogue of books and to be placed on our mailing list, please send us this card.

PLEASE PRINT

Book in which this card was found _____

NAME _____

ADDRESS _____

CITY _____ STATE _____

ZIP / POSTAL CODE _____ COUNTRY _____

pilot claimed it would be only a few minutes, Dayle dragged me off the plane. We re-rented a car, broke into our old apartment through the window, and stayed put for about a week. We found out later that the plane was delayed, not for a few minutes, but for about ten hours.

Then there was the time we were in Los Angeles, filming at the Paramount Studios. Driving peacefully along Melrose Avenue on the way to the Los Angeles International Airport, I was in the left lane ready to make my left turn toward LAX. Then, just like radar, Dayle got this flash.

"Turn right!" she shouted.

Errrrrrrr . . . I turned, cutting across three lanes of traffic without getting into an accident. I quickly turned right onto Crescent Heights Boulevard. Now we were on our way to the Burbank Airport.

I turned to Dayle and asked, "Why are we doing this?"

She replied, "I want to save time. If we go to L.A. Airport, we might miss our flight. If we go to Burbank, I know we won't miss the flight."

That sounded logical.

We ended up at the Burbank airport, with plenty of time to spare.

To tell you the truth, our luck isn't any better while traveling on a cruise ship. I remember our first wedding anniversary; we had booked ourselves on the American Hawaiian Cruise ship. The night we were to board, it was monsooning. We boarded early and went to the galley to have a nice, pleasant meal.

Right smack in the middle of dinner, Dayle stared at me with that funny look of hers. Oh, oh, here we go again! I dropped my fork; I knew exactly what she was going to say. But this time I was smart. I yelled, "We are *not* leaving this ship till I finish my $550 dinner. And that's final!"

Several days later we found out that the ship encountered enormous waves and never docked in Kauai.

Life with Dayle always seems to end up like an episode out of *I Love Lucy*. Of course, I'm Ricky and she's Lucy. Never a dull moment.

I remember the time we were living peacefully in Hawaii. We didn't have a care in the world; everything was wonderful. Then President Bush declared war on Iraq. My wife held her hands to her cheeks in dismay as she watched the President on television.

"Blythe, go get the passports, and sell everything in the house; we're moving to Canada." Here we go again. We didn't move to Canada, but my wife bought a house sight unseen in Lake Tahoe. Guess what, folks, I'm writing this chapter in Lake Tahoe. Always remember, if you marry a Psychic, be prepared for anything.

Speaking of Lake Tahoe, I married a human barometer. In the summer of 1992, I noticed my wife stocking up an enormous amount of canned goods. Our grocery bill was well over $200. Then, in the middle of the summer, she decided to order seven cords of firewood—a bit much, I thought. Then she bought a brand new, huge snowblower. I was beginning to question her sanity.

"Dayle, do you expect a lot of snow or something?" I asked politely.

As winter closed in, Dayle ran out and bought a short-wave radio so she could listen to the weather reports. One day we drove to Carson City to go grocery shopping. She bought thirty-five bags of groceries at three different grocery stores! Three days later, the biggest storm in ten years slammed into Lake Tahoe. The next thing I knew, we had neighbors from all over the place wanting to buy food from us. Would you believe that the grocery stores ran out of food, because the roads were closed and the trucks were unable to make their deliveries. That winter we had over forty feet of snow, and I was still shoveling snow two months later.

Now I pay attention when my wife begins to act strangely. I've also noticed something new: whenever her arm aches, a few days later, blizzard-like conditions occur. Well, at least we always know when to stock up on food and canned goods. My wife's arm is much more accurate than the local weatherman. I could go on and on. The above stories are just a few examples of the exciting and unpredictable life I lead with my wife.

CHAPTER 22

THE PSYCHIC WITHIN ME

Each and every one of us has a Psychic within, one who is sensitive to other people's feelings. The New Age movement isn't new at all; in fact, it's very old. Psychics date back since before Biblical times. The Old Testament mentions Psychics and prophets who did miraculous things. Stories throughout the Bible tell of great kings who would not make a move without consulting their prophets or astrologers. In those days the prophets had better be right, or they would have been put to death. That is why so many of the Biblical prophecies were made so many years in the future, sometimes fifty years or more. There was absolutely no way to check the accuracy of the prophets until after their deaths. Some of the Biblical prophecies are still coming true today.

I recall growing up as a child in New Jersey and knowing that I was different. Something inside of me yearned to help others. I didn't know there were words for the experiences I had, such as *telepathy* for the reading of the mind. I actually thought I had discovered mind-reading all by myself. I knew that normal children didn't know the same things I knew. Yet, there was no one out there who could help me understand what I was thinking. I remember I liked the space I was in. I was the perpetual dreamer.

As a child I was fascinated by the future. I look back now and realize I never lived in the past or the present; I was extremely futuristic. The pain of my childhood contributed to most of my Psychic ability. Genetics played a large part, but nothing, my friend, could erase my horror stories of the past, the horror stories I wrote about in my first book, *Dare to Be Different!*

Years later, I would pick up books and find meanings and definitions for the things I already knew. It seemed to me that when I looked at reality in a different way, I was considered unusual or crazy by the majority of people. Well, that was me.

My mother called me "the gifted one," while some children made fun of me and others ran away. If I only knew then about the abuse of being a Psychic child, I don't think I would have chosen this path. The pain of growing up in a different world is beyond what you could imagine.

I always was fascinated by the future. I always believed that there was more to life than what could be seen or touched. I knew there was more out there. In my quest, I was determined to find the answers.

After years of training myself, reading books, practicing reading cards, and reading people for free, I was about to embark on a new adventure. I had to train myself through trial and error. Life was my teacher. I graduated from the school of hard knocks, and I deserved every notch I carved for myself.

I recall always knowing in my teens as to when I would be fired from a job. I never knew why. I found out years later that I was simply reading the mind of my boss. I always had premonitions of plane crashes or car accidents, and they all would come true. It seemed to me I was an unguided missile. I needed someone to help me find my way. The teenage years were rough—moving from town to town, living in different cities, never having roots. I married young. Those were my formative years.

The year must have been 1969 when everything went amok. I remember being married to Bob and living in Los Angeles. My Psychic ability began to soar; yet, I was out of control. It was at this stage in my life that every single thing I envisioned happened. If I had a vision of a plane crash, it would happen. If I saw a friend getting into an accident, that also would occur. My ability was surging and I didn't know what to do. I thought I was going mad. That seemed to have been another turning point in my life.

Throughout the years I have known many Psychics, and there is always one thing we have in common, *a turning point in our lives.* That's when an awakening in life occurs, usually during a crisis, such as a death in the family or a divorce, something so traumatic that one is forced to awaken. There's always something that triggers the Psychic ability to emerge more so than usual. I've yet to figure this out logically: it takes a *crisis* in our lives, which triggers an emotional response, which triggers ESP to occur. It's at this point that a Psychic chooses to seek help and finesse his or her ability. If no help is to be found, one can read books to learn and understand. Of course, in my time there were hardly any books to explain what I was going through. This crisis can cause one to become off-balanced, even crazy! But if one gets a grip on life, the Psychic ability will emerge. I somehow was not going to let my ability control me. I decided to be in control of my mind.

I began reading positive mental attitude books, learning to understand ESP through trial and error. The problem I faced with ESP was religion. I thought at one point I was being possessed, a very common deduction. I learned later that ESP had *nothing* to do with religion, that ESP is just a function in a portion of the brain that we don't yet understand.

There was and still is a great misconception that if you are Psychic you must be evil. This saddens me. *Education* is the key to understanding the unknown. The words *supernatural* and *paranormal* are also misleading and cause general misconceptions about psychic phenomena. I discovered that there is usually fear when there is lack of knowledge. When knowledge is acquired, the fear is removed. If only people would take the time to explore the unlimited powers of the mind, they would realize how universal these powers are.

As I educated myself slowly, I realized I was more gifted than most others I knew in the field of ESP. One day I decided to pick up my tarot cards and learn more about them. What I saw in the cards amazed me. Reading cards for free just didn't pay the bills, so I decided once again to get a job and join the ranks of the working world.

I got a job at a fitness center in an elite section of town. My job as a front office receptionist for the stars of Hollywood was considered a glamour job. Why, I met Elvis, Glenn Ford, Rob Reiner— every star imaginable. This was the first job I loved with a passion. On my break I could use the gym with a star such as Michelle Lee. I entered into conversations with many of the movie stars, but often I was lost for words. So, on my break, I would ask the stars if they wanted their fortunes read. Of course they were more than interested.

Word quickly got around. I guess this was my only way of making friends. The next thing I knew, on every break some television or movie star would be asking me to give a reading. Within weeks I was getting popular. This was one job I did not want to lose.

But Blue Monday came around. I was on my lunch hour and my husband Bob was using the gym for the first time. I came back from lunch and found someone sitting at my desk answering the phones. I asked the supervisor, "Who's that girl sitting in my chair?" The supervisor politely told me I had been replaced. It seems the company thought I had wonderful sales ability; they were going to promote me to a higher position. I explained to my supervisor that I didn't want to be promoted; I wanted my old job back. A few moments later I rehashed this whole conversation in my mind and decided to go on a break to sort things out. I left the office and phoned Bob in the gym. "Bob, you better get the hell out of there! I've just quit my job."

Several days later, the supervisor came to my apartment with her husband. She begged me to come back to work. "Not unless I get my old job back," I replied.

"Sorry, Dayle, it's out of my hands. Either you take a position in sales, or you'll have to look for another job," she said. I was heartbroken. She added, "I hear you've been doing readings."

"Is that why I was fired?" I asked.

"No, we felt you were too good to be a front office receptionist." She smiled.

"There's nothing wrong with being a receptionist." I said. I realized there was no point in arguing with her; besides, we were good friends.

She said, "Oh, well, since I can't convince you to come back to work, would you mind reading my husband's cards?"

"No, not at all," I replied. I sat them down and asked her husband to shuffle the cards. The visions passed rapidly by my eyes. The feelings were overwhelming.

I looked up at her and said, "Your husband is going to be very famous, you know. I see him making films; it looks like a short film. He will win an award for this film. *I know* I will watch him on television winning this award."

"That's very interesting," she replied. "My husband is just starting to work on his own documentary."

"Well, looks like you have a bright future. Fame is your lot," I said.

Approximately seven years later, my husband Bob was watching the Academy Awards on television. "Dayle," he said excitedly, "that man on television—you predicted he would win an award years ago. Look at this! Come here, take a look. He just won an award for *The Man Who Skied Mount Everest*."

"Son of a gun, you're right, Bob. I remember telling him I would watch him win an award. I guess I should stick to card reading." We both laughed.

It wasn't until my early thirties that I decided to embark on becoming a full-time Psychic. My path was already chosen for me. I started off on a local radio station in Lake Tahoe, which led to radio and television in Hawaii. Hawaii is where my fame and spirituality began. It was there I first worked on missing persons, murders, and finding lost dogs and children. Through my gift I even saved a few lives. I loved my work. I loved helping people. I realized I had a quest.

I've studied ESP for well over twenty-five years. But for all the knowledge I have obtained, I've only scratched the surface. There's more out there than meets the eye. I realize there is much more knowledge than the average person could ever understand in a lifetime.

These days I am devoting my life to helping people. I figure that when I die, my Maker will at least say, "Hey, Dayle, you've done good!" Here on earth, it's an occasional thank you for helping to save someone's life.

I've tried many times to give up my work. I've wanted to run and hide from the public. But there is always someone out there who needs help; I always run into someone who is crying uncontrollably. Silly me, I always go to the rescue.

I've been told this job has been chosen for me. I've even been told that I chose this work in another life. I don't know, but I'll venture to say that if someone dropped a couple of million in my lap, I would run and hide from this job. However, with my luck, I would more likely give the money away to the needy and go on helping mankind.

I pray that the field will become more legitimate in my lifetime. I hope I can contribute to that. Meanwhile, through education and through my writings, in the future I hope to enlighten more than a few souls.

ABOUT THE AUTHOR

Psychic Dayle Schear was born in Newark, New Jersey, the youngest of two daughters, but soon Dayle's parents moved the family to Los Angeles.

While growing up in Los Angeles, Dayle more fully realized her Psychic potential when she randomly picked up a deck of Tarot cards. She studied the cards for ten years and devoted many years to giving free readings and helping people. She learned, over a period of time, that most everything she told people had come true.

Inevitably, the world-famed Psychic, Peter Hurkos, discovered Dayle's talent. Following their encounter, she underwent six years of vigorous training with Peter until his death. Dayle is his "only living protege."

In 1987, Dayle married a local boy from the Hawaiian Islands, Blythe Arakawa. Together with their prize possessions—German shepherds—they divide their time between Honolulu, Hawaii and Lake Tahoe.

Dayle is also the author of *Dare to be Different!*, which describes the eventful, spiritual journey of a Psychic, and, soon to be released, *Tarot for the Beginner* (Blue Dolphin 1994). Another book, *What If?*, a spiritual journey into one's mind, is forthcoming.

Dayle lectures throughout the United States on E.S.P. She has an on-going television talk show called "E.S.P. & You" on a Honolulu CBS affiliate which airs several times a year, and, in her spare time, she is a guest on numerous radio talk shows.

She has worked for U.S. Navy intelligence in Hawaii, and with law enforcement agencies throughout the country and abroad. Dayle specializes in Psychometry: the art of holding on to objects to see into the past, present, and future. Through these gifts she has been able to solve numerous murder cases, as well as find missing children. Her special gift is helping people on a one-to-one basis.

While relaxing, Dayle and Blythe enjoy travel and playing with their German shepherds, as well as boating on Lake Tahoe and around the Hawaiian Islands.

If you want to address the author, write to Dayle Schear, P.O. Box 172, Zephyr Cove, NV 89448, or call (702) 588-3337.

BOOKS AND TAPES by PSYCHIC DAYLE SCHEAR

Dare to Be Different! (soft cover)	$16.00
The Psychic Within	$14.95
Tarot for the Beginner: Learn to Read the Tarot Cards in One Hour or Less (book)	$ 6.95
Tarot for the Beginner (video)	$19.95
Tarot for the Beginner (book & video)	$24.95
What If? (book, forthcoming)	

BEST-SELLING BOOKS from BLUE DOLPHIN PUBLISHING

Mary's Message to the World, Annie Kirkwood	$12.95
Are You Really Too Sensitive?: How to Develop and Understand Your Sensitivity as the Strength It Is, Marcy Calhoun	$12.95
Beyond Boundaries: The Adventures of a Seer, Louise Hauck	$12.95
The Boss Should Be a Woman: How Women Can Manage Their Way to the Top and Compromise Nothing, Jack McAllen	$12.95
Prince Charming Lives! Finding the Love of Your Life, Phyllis Light	$12.95
Your Dream Relationship: Eleven Steps to Finding Unconditional Love, Alix & Ron Gavran	$10.00
Points: The Most Practical Program Ever to Improve Your Self-Image, Dave Gustafson	$12.95
Love, Hope & Recovery: Healing the Pain of Addiction, Joann Breeden	$12.95
Love to Be Happy: The Secrets of Sustainable Joy, Mehdi Bahadori	$10.95
Survival Guide for the New Millennium: How to Survive the Coming Earth Changes, Byron Kirkwood	$ 8.95
Mission to Millboro, Marge Rieder	$13.00
Dolphin Divination Cards (boxed set of 108 cards), Nancy Clemens	$ 9.00

SubTotal _____

10% discount for book orders of 5 or more!

Tax (7.25% CA only) _____

Shipping _____

TOTAL _____

Order directly from Blue Dolphin Publishing: **1 (800) 643-0765**
Mastercard, Visa, or Personal Check
Shipping Charges: $3.00 for the first book, $1.00 for each additional book
Please add sales tax (California only): 7.25% on book(s) total
Orders are shipped bookrate within 48 hours
Or Mail to: Blue Dolphin Publishing, P.O. Box 1920, Nevada City, CA 95959

☐ Please write to be placed on our mailing list for new books and tapes